THE ESSENTIAL

Instant Pot®

COOKBOOK

THE ESSENTIAL

Instant Pot®

COOKBOOK

Fresh and foolproof recipes for
your electric pressure cooker

Coco Morante

TEN SPEED PRESS
California | New York

Contents

Introduction

The Instant Pot—an electric, programmable pressure cooker—has quickly become one of the most popular kitchen appliances on the market. If you grew up with a traditional stove-top pressure cooker, you'll be amazed at how far pressure cooking has come.

Gone are the days of the scary, rocking pressure regulator on stove-top models. The Instant Pot is whisper quiet while it cooks foods under pressure. It's also extremely versatile. With a wide range of programmable settings, it does the job of a traditional pressure cooker as well as a slow cooker, rice cooker, and yogurt maker.

Indeed, the range of foods you can cook in the Instant Pot is nothing short of mind-blowing. It'll turn out both a pot of chili and the loaf of cornbread to go alongside it, a kid-friendly macaroni and cheese that's ready in a snap, and a silky-smooth cheesecake that will be the envy of every home baker.

This cookbook will tell you how to make those dishes and more. It includes seven chapters of recipes that range from globally inspired dishes to retro American classics with modern updates. You'll also find how-to instructions for such staples as rice, beans, and broth, as well as directions for flavor-boosting add-ins to keep in the freezer for fast weeknight cooking from scratch.

Once you are comfortable with all of the buttons on the Instant Pot, you'll discover that using it is much like cooking in a pot on the stove. It has settings to sauté and brown (especially useful when starting soups, stews, and braises), to pressure steam (great for getting vegetables done fast), and even to make yogurt. Plus, once a dish has finished cooking, the Instant Pot will keep it warm for up to 10 hours.

I've done my best to include a broad array of recipes to please omnivores and vegetarians alike, as well as folks who are staying gluten-free or dairy-free. There are dishes for breakfast, lunch, and dinner, and for luscious desserts and between-meal snacks. And I've tested every recipe in my own kitchen to make sure it is not only foolproof but also delicious.

When I wrote these recipes, I wanted them to be both intuitive and easy to follow. To make sure I've delivered on that goal, I have included clear instructions at every step so you'll never have to guess which button to press. Decoding the buttons is the main hurdle to learning how to use the Instant Pot, and I've eliminated that obstacle in this book. You're bound to get the hang of things after making just a handful of dishes, and using the Instant Pot will soon be as second nature as stove-top cooking.

Whether you're new to the Instant Pot or just looking for new tips and tricks, the introductory pages that follow will help get you started.

How to Use the Instant Pot

When you first take your Instant Pot out of the box, do yourself a favor and immediately open the manual and turn to the diagrams. They'll help you get acquainted with the different parts of the Instant Pot, including all of the buttons and light-up indicators on the front and the mechanisms of the lid.

I've tested these recipes in four models of Instant Pot: the LUX60 V3, DUO60, DUO60 Plus, and Ultra. The DUO and Ultra models are my favorites, as they have a handy notch for resting the lid when the pot is open. They also include a setting for culturing yogurt, which the LUX models do not.

If you are primarily cooking for four people or fewer, I'd go with one of the "60" models, all of which have a 6-quart capacity. If you plan to cook larger pieces of meat (over 4 pounds) or serve a larger crowd on a regular basis, go with the DUO80, which has an 8-quart capacity. If you're using an 8-quart model, you may need to scale some recipes up to include at least 1½ cups of liquid so that the pot can successfully come to pressure.

No matter which model of Instant Pot you have, the panel on the front has buttons for cooking different kinds of foods, adjusting the pot to high or low pressure, regulating the temperature of certain settings, and setting the cooking time. There is also an LED display that lets you know when the pot is on or off and how much time is left on the program setting once the pot reaches pressure.

This chart below shows what program settings are available on each Instant Pot model. The number in the name of each model corresponds with its size.

Cooking Program	LUX60	LUX60 V3	DUO50/60/80	DUO60 Plus	Ultra	SMART
Manual/Pressure Cook	x	x	x	x	x	x
Soup/Broth	x	x	x	x	x	x
Meat/Stew	x	x	x	x	x	x
Poultry	x		x			x
Bean/Chili	x	x	x	x	x	x
Cake		x		x	x	
Egg		x		x	x	
Sauté	x	x	x	x	x	x
Rice	x	x	x	x	x	x
Multigrain	x	x	x	x	x	x
Steam	x	x	x	x	x	x
Porridge	x	x	x	x	x	x
Slow Cook	x	x	x	x	x	x
Yogurt			x	x	x	x
Sterilize				x	x	

Function (aka Cooking Program) Keys

You'll select a function key depending on what sort of food you are cooking. In Instant Pot terminology, this translates to pressing a function key to select its cooking program. For example, you'll press the Soup/Broth key to cook a soup, the Rice key to steam a pot of rice, and so on. Each pressure cooking program can be adjusted to High or Low pressure, as well as Less, Normal, or More cooking time (shown in minutes on the LED display), with Normal being the default setting. You can also adjust the time up or down manually in any setting with the + and - buttons (although the Ultra has a central dial). Here's a rundown of all the cooking program buttons (the chart opposite shows which ones are on each model).

MANUAL/PRESSURE COOK You can cook any pressure cooker recipe on the Manual setting. If you're interested in using recipes written for stove-top pressure cookers, this setting is handy, as those recipes can easily be cooked in the Instant Pot. It opens up a whole world of recipes for you to explore, not just ones specifically meant for the Instant Pot. Stove-top cookers cook faster because they operate at slightly higher pressures, so add 15 percent to the cooking time of the Instant Pot. Depending on the model of Instant Pot you have, you'll use the Adjust or Pressure Level button to toggle between the Low Pressure and High Pressure settings.

SOUP/BROTH The heat ramps up a little more gently on this setting than on the previous setting, which makes it good for simmering soups and broths. Even better, broths turn out clear, not cloudy, when they're cooked under pressure. You'll find recipes for beef bone broth and low-sodium chicken broth in the Pantry chapter.

MEAT/STEW This one is self-explanatory. Adjust the time to Less, Normal, or More, depending on whether you like your meat cooked soft, very soft, or falling off the bone.

BEAN/CHILI Whether you're cooking a basic pot of beans (page 30), Indian dal, or chili, use this cooking program. Adjust the cooking time to Less for just-done beans, Normal for soft beans, or More for very soft beans. See the chart on page 160 for exact cooking times for a variety of beans.

CAKE Use the Less, Normal, and More settings according to the recipe you are making, from delicate sponge cake to dense pound cake to cheesecake.

EGG You can cook soft-, medium-, or hard-boiled eggs. The Less, Normal, and More settings are timed for extra-large eggs, so adjust the cooking times up or down as needed if your eggs are a different size.

SAUTÉ Unlike a slow cooker, the Instant Pot allows you to simmer, sauté, and sear foods before cooking them under pressure. This is not a pressure setting, and you should never put the locking lid on when you're using it. I occasionally use a tempered glass lid (either the one from Instant Pot or one I already have that fits the pot) on this setting when I want to sweat vegetables or simmer delicate dumplings.

RICE Any type of white rice can be cooked on this setting. The Less, Normal, and More settings will yield just tender, tender, and soft rice, respectively.

MULTIGRAIN The moderate, even heat of the Multigrain setting is perfect for brown rice and other long-cooking grains. The More setting includes a warm, 45-minute presoak before an hour of pressure cooking and is well suited to mixtures of tough grains and beans.

STEAM The Instant Pot comes with a trivet that is used for raising foods off the bottom of the pot for steaming under pressure. You can also use any wire-mesh, silicone, or metal steamer basket.

PORRIDGE Use this setting when making congee (rice porridge), oatmeal, or a porridge made of any beans and/or other grains. Always use the natural release method when making porridge and never fill the pot more than half full to avoid a spattered mess. Cooking porridge under pressure is perfectly safe as long as you stick to those guidelines.

SLOW COOK The Instant Pot doesn't just pressure cook. It also slow cooks. If you come across a great new slow cooker recipe or have some old slow cooker favorites that you'd like to make, use this setting. The Less, Normal, and More settings on the Instant Pot correspond to the Low, Medium, and High settings on a slow cooker. For easier cleanup, use a tempered glass lid (either the one available from Instant Pot or any lid that fits on the pot).

YOGURT This setting has two yogurt-related functions: it sterilizes milk on the More setting and then turns the milk into yogurt on the Normal setting. Homemade yogurt is easy to make and more economical than store-bought. You can even culture the yogurt right in a glass container inside the pot with my method on page 156. This is my preferred way to make yogurt, since it goes from Instant Pot to fridge with zero cleanup.

STERILIZE If you like to make jams and jellies or plan on canning other high-acid foods, you'll be able to save space on the stove top and avoid a big hot-water bath by using the Instant Pot. The Normal setting sterilizes at about 110°C (230°F), and the More setting sterilizes at about 115°C (240°F).

Operation Keys

These are the buttons that adjust the pressure, cooking time, and, in certain cases, the heat level of whatever cooking program you've selected. Most Instant Pot models have an Adjust button that toggles among the Less, Normal, and More time and heat settings. For pressure settings, it adjusts the time, and for non-pressure settings, including Yogurt, Slow Cook, and Sauté, it adjusts the heat level. The + and - buttons adjust the cooking time up and down, respectively.

The DUO60 Plus has a dedicated Pressure level button instead of Adjust and/or Pressure buttons, and you press the appropriate function key more than once to toggle among the Less, Normal, and More time and heat settings. The LUX60 model pressure cooks at High Pressure only. It does not have a Low Pressure setting.

DELAY START If you have the LUX60 V3, DUO60 Plus, or Ultra, you can delay the start of the cooking time for a recipe. You won't find many uses for this function, as you typically won't want to leave perishable foods in the Instant Pot for any length of time before cooking them. The one task I do like this function for is soaking and cooking beans. I'll put my beans and water in the pot, delay the time for 8 to 12 hours, and then wake up to perfectly cooked beans in the morning.

MODE AND FUNCTION INDICATORS These are the lights that turn on to indicate what mode (low or high pressure) or function (aka cooking program) is currently selected on the Instant Pot. All of the function keys and mode indicators have a little white circle that lights up when they are selected.

KEY WARM/CANCEL This multipurpose button has two separate functions: it cancels any cooking program, and it puts the pot on the Keep Warm setting, similar to the warming setting on a slow cooker. The DUO60 Plus, DUO60, and Ultra models have separate buttons for the Keep Warm and Cancel functions.

The Lid and Releasing Pressure

Now that you know the basic terminology for everything on the front panel of the pot, let's talk about the lid. The lids of the various Instant Pot models (LUX, DUO, SMART, and Ultra) all look slightly different, but they have similar mechanisms.

Pressure/Steam Release

The Pressure Release, also called Steam Release on some models, can be set to two positions, Sealing or Venting. When the pot is closed and the Pressure Release is set to Sealing, the pot can come up to pressure. When the cooking program is finished, you can move the Pressure Release to Venting to release the steam from the pot, making it safe to open. And it's okay if the Pressure Release jiggles a bit or seems as if it is not fully secured. It's supposed to feel that way. You can remove it for cleaning as well.

Quick Release vs. Natural Pressure Release

You can release the pressure on the Instant Pot in three different ways:

1. Quick Release: The moment the cooking program finishes, move the Pressure Release to Venting. This will cause a forceful plume of steam to issue forth, releasing the pressure from the Instant Pot. Use this method for delicate foods that require just a few minutes of cooking, like steamed vegetables.

2. Natural Pressure Release: Rather than moving the Pressure Release, do nothing. Once a cooking program finishes, the pot will eventually lose pressure on its own as it cools. This can take anywhere from a few minutes to 30 minutes or more. That's because the pot retains more or less heat and pressure depending on the volume of food inside. The pot automatically defaults to its Keep Warm setting at the end of a cooking program, and you can leave it for up to 10 hours before it will shut off completely.

3. Combination: I often wait 10 or 15 minutes after the end of a cooking program, then move the Pressure Release to Venting to release a less geyser-like amount of steam from the pot.

Sealing Ring

The only part of the lid that you'll likely have to replace eventually is the silicone sealing ring, which is seated in a rack inside the perimeter of the lid. It has a life of 6 to 18 months, depending on how frequently you use your Instant Pot. The sealing ring needs to be seated properly in the lid for the pot to come up to pressure, so make sure to replace it securely in the sealing ring rack after you've cleaned it. I keep separate sealing rings for sweet and savory foods because the ring can retain strong odors.

Anti-Block Shield

The little metal cap that fits on the inner part of the exhaust valve on the underside of the lid is the anti-block shield. It helps to keep foamy foods from blocking the valve. It's good practice to remove it and clean it after each use of the pot.

The Pressure Cooker Pantry

Pressure cooking is unique in that you need a fair amount of liquid for recipes to work properly, but very little moisture evaporates from the food as it cooks. I use a few secret ingredients in my recipes to help amp up flavor and absorb moisture. Here are my favorites.

BROTH CONCENTRATES AND BOUILLON This is an incredibly convenient way to add flavor. My preferred brands are the organic offerings from Better Than Bouillon and the curry cubes from Edward & Sons. I also like the Beef Bone Broth concentrate from Kitchen Accomplice; it's the only commercial beef broth I use because it doesn't have the tinny taste of many store-bought broths. When I don't have homemade broth on hand, I reach for these products.

DRIED FRUITS AND VEGETABLES Dehydrated foods soak up excess liquids, so they're a no-brainer in pressure cooker recipes. Add a handful of raisins or chopped dried apples to applesauce (page 157), and it will thicken as it cools. Dried mushrooms are a great addition to soups and stews, and sun-dried tomatoes perk up pasta dishes and braises.

GRAINS AND BEANS I make lots of one-pot dishes with chicken and rice, so I always keep a few different types of rice on hand. Oatmeal is a morning staple, which means steel-cut oats are in my pantry at all times. Beans are a popular choice in my kitchen, too, and I usually have chickpeas for Hummus (page 33), *gigantes* or large lima beans for side dishes, and lentils for soups and Vegan Sloppy Joes (page 36) on hand.

HERB AND SPICE BLENDS Spice blends are great for perking up pressure-cooked dishes. I use all kinds of them in my cooking, from common ones like chili powder and Italian seasoning to herbes de Provence, North African *ras el hanout*, Jamaican jerk seasoning, and Ethiopian *berbere*. Pick up your choices at the grocery store or visit a well-stocked spice shop where you can sniff before you buy. Some of my favorite purveyors are Oaktown Spice Shop in Oakland, California; World Spice Merchants in Seattle, Washington; and Penzeys, with locations throughout the United States.

TOMATO PASTE This concentrated form of tomatoes adds body and depth of flavor to tomato-based dishes, so if you're using tomatoes (fresh or canned), double up on the flavor by adding a big dollop of tomato paste as well. Because it can be difficult to get through a can of tomato paste before it goes bad, I like to freeze it in 1-tablespoon dollops for later use.

WORCESTERSHIRE SAUCE AND OTHER STRONGLY FLAVORED CONDIMENTS These are great when you need an umami flavor bomb to perk up a recipe. They'll improve chilis, stews, and braised meat dishes, making them extra savory. Dijon mustard is another go-to flavor enhancer of mine, as well as soy sauce, tamari, coconut aminos, fish sauce, and miso paste.

Must-Have Tools

These are my favorite accessories for the Instant Pot. Most are available at any well-stocked cookware store or can be purchased online.

SILICONE MINI MITTS are perfect for lifting the inner pot in and out of the Instant Pot housing or moving the Pressure Release, as they protect fingers from the jet of steam.

AN EXTRA INNER POT is nice to have around if you plan on cooking two Instant Pot dishes in one night and don't want to wash a pot between recipes.

TEMPERED GLASS LIDS are available for all of the Instant Pot models, and they're nice for using on the Slow Cook or Sauté settings.

A WIRE-MESH, SILICONE, OR EXPANDABLE METAL STEAMER BASKET is necessary for steaming vegetables in the Instant Pot.

THE STAINLESS-STEEL TRIVET that comes with your Instant Pot is perfect for pot-in-pot (PIP) cooking tasks like making cheesecakes, frittatas, and other foods that cook in a separate pan or dish *inside* the inner pot (see page 157). It's also great for pressure-steaming whole chickens or big cuts of meat, as it keeps them out of the steaming liquid and you can use it to lift them out of the pot.

KITCHEN TONGS are indispensable since everything cooks in a deep pot, so they are perfect for getting in there to turn and toss ingredients around.

A FLEXIBLE TURNER is ideal for getting under meat patties, chicken pieces, and other foods that can stick a bit when you sear them in the pot.

JAR LIFTERS AND JAM FUNNELS are especially useful if you're making yogurt, jam, or anything that needs to be ladled into jars, cooked in the pot, and then retrieved from the pot once it's ready.

KITCHEN THERMOMETERS are indispensable and great for checking the internal temperature of meat or poultry to ensure it is cooked through. A probe thermometer with a remote display is useful when making yogurt, as you can set it to beep when it's time to add the culture to the cooled milk.

SEVEN-INCH ROUND PANS AND DISHES are the perfect size for placing inside the 6-quart Instant Pot. I use a 7-inch springform pan for cheesecakes; a 7-cup round Pyrex container for omelets, crustless quiches, and bread puddings; and a 7-inch round cake pan with 3-inch sides for cakes and breads. A 1½-quart soufflé dish also works well. If you have the 8-quart Instant Pot, use 8-inch round pans.

A FAT SEPARATOR (AKA GRAVY SEPARATOR) is pressed into service almost every time I'm cooking meat in the Instant Pot. I pour the cooking liquid through the strainer of the separator, let the fat rise, and then pour the defatted liquid back into the pot to reduce, thicken, or blend into a sauce.

SILICONE MUFFIN PANS AND MINI LOAF PANS are good for holding prepped ingredients before they are added to the pot and for freezing broth (page 154 and 155), Italian *soffrito* for soups and stews (page 149), Puerto Rican *sofrito* for Arroz con Pollo (page 64), and leftovers in small portions. Just freeze the food solid in the silicone pan, then pop it out, transfer it to ziplock plastic freezer bags, label the bags with the date and contents, and store the bags in the freezer.

How to Convert Recipes for the Instant Pot

Step 1: Calibrate your expectations. Whole chickens will not emerge from the Instant Pot with burnished, crispy skin. Large cuts of meat will still take some time to cook through and become tender (though much less time than if you braise them on the stove top or in the oven). Delicate vegetables like asparagus won't stay tender-crisp on the Keep Warm setting all day.

Step 2: Make sure the recipe is Instant Pot–friendly. If it's a soup, stew, or braise, chances are you'll be able to make it in the Instant Pot. Avoid fast-cooking dishes like seared chicken cutlets, delicate fish fillets, and high-heat stir-fries. Instead, take advantage of the pot's recognized ability to make tough cuts of meat tender, steam grains and vegetables more quickly, and cook just about anything without drying it out.

Step 3: Adjust the amount of liquid in the recipe. If you're braising, you will need only about 1 cup of liquid for the pot to come up to pressure (sometimes less if you are using vegetables that release a lot of liquid as they cook). Soups and sauces won't reduce while they're pressure cooking, so don't use more liquid than you want to end up with in the finished recipe. If you have too much liquid at the end of cooking, you can always reduce it on the Sauté setting. I find that for every 15 minutes on the Sauté setting, about 1 cup of liquid evaporates from the uncovered pot.

Step 4: Read through the recipe steps to figure out which function keys you'll need to press. If the recipe includes a simmering, sautéing, searing, or browning step, use the Sauté setting. For most models of Instant Pots, you'll press the Adjust button to select the Less, Normal, or More heat setting. On the DUO60 Plus model, you'll press the Sauté button itself to change the heat setting.

For the main portion of the cooking, choose the cooking program that corresponds to the type of food in the recipe, such as Meat/Stew for a pot roast or Bean/Chili for a pot of beans. If none of them seems like a perfect match, use the Manual or Pressure Cook setting.

Step 5: Determine the cooking time. Scan the ingredients list for the longest-cooking ingredient in the recipe, then consult the charts in this book or on the Instant Pot website to determine the cooking time.

Step 6: Decide whether to perform a quick release or a natural pressure release. For steamed dishes, a quick release is usually the best option. For dishes that can produce foam (grains, beans, or simmered fruit sauces), I always let the pressure release naturally. For in-between dishes, such as soups, stews, and braises, I generally let the pressure release for 10 or 15 minutes before moving the Pressure Release to Venting.

Step 7: Make your recipe and enjoy!

Troubleshooting and FAQ

What follows is a series of questions I get asked all the time about cooking in the Instant Pot. If I haven't answered your question or if your question isn't here, get in touch with Instant Pot directly.

Q: What's the small, clear plastic cuplike thing that comes with the Instant Pot?

A: It is a condensation collector and designed to catch any water that collects in the lid reservoir, so that it doesn't drop onto your countertop.

Q: I selected one of the cooking programs, but nothing is happening! What's going on?

A: When you press a function key, it gives you about 10 seconds of lag time so you can adjust the time, pressure, or heat setting. After that, it will beep to let you know the cooking program has started (on the Ultra, you'll have to press the Start button). If you're using a pressure setting, the pot will come up to pressure and then display the cooking time in minutes, counting down until the cooking program finishes. At that point, the pot will beep ten times in a row and default to its Keep Warm setting. The LED display will count up from the time the cooking program ended to indicate how long the food has been keeping warm.

Q: How do I adjust the cooking time? How do I adjust the pressure setting?

A: Once you have selected a cooking program with one of the function keys, use the + and - buttons to adjust the cooking time up or down. On most models, the Adjust button will toggle the pressure setting between the High Pressure and Low Pressure settings. The DUO Plus has a Pressure Level button, and the Ultra has a central dial that is used to select and toggle between all of the pot's modes and functions. If you've selected a non-pressure setting such as Sauté, the Adjust button allows you to toggle the heat setting among Less, Normal, and More. On models without an Adjust button, press the function key itself or use the central dial.

Q: Why did my food take way longer than 15 minutes to cook when I set it to 15 minutes?

A: If you're using pressure cooking settings, the cooking time counts down from when the pot gets up to pressure. Depending on the volume and temperature of the food you're cooking, it can take anywhere from a few minutes to 30 minutes to reach the desired pressure (large volumes of food and frozen foods take longer). You may also need to allow extra time if you are letting the pot release pressure naturally, which can take a fair amount of time if you're cooking a big batch of food.

Q: Can I cook a whole frozen chicken, a 4-pound beef roast, or other big block of rock-solid, nowhere-near-thawed meat in the Instant Pot?

A: The short answer is no, it's not a good idea. You're better off making something else for dinner and letting the frozen meat thaw for a day or two before you cook it. The long answer is plan ahead next time and cut the meat into thin slices (or shape ground meat into meatballs) before you freeze it. It will thaw a lot faster that way, and in a pinch you can cook it straight from frozen, too! Just add a few minutes to the recommended cooking time if you're using frozen meat. For more information on cooking frozen meat, see page 83.

Q: My Instant Pot never sealed! What happened?

A: The pot requires enough steam build-up to come to pressure. When it comes to pressure, the float valve lifts up and the pot seals. There are several reasons the pot may not have sealed. Here are the most likely possibilities. Did you . . .

- clean the lid well, including the sealing gasket?
- use enough liquid in the recipe (1 cup or so)?
- leave out any thickeners like flour or cornstarch?
- avoid layering pieces of meat on top of rice, covering it completely?
- make sure the sealing ring wasn't warped and that it was seated properly?
- set the Pressure Release to the Sealing position?
- make sure a cooking program was selected, and the LED display on the pot read "On"?
- fill the pot half full or less for starchy foods, or two-thirds full or less for soups and stews?

If you answered yes to all of these questions, then you've got me stumped! It's time to contact the Instant Pot company directly for assistance.

Q: Why won't my Instant Pot open?

A: The pot lid has a safety mechanism that prevents you from opening the pot when it is cooking under pressure. The pressure needs to be fully released before the lid can be lifted off. If the pot is completely quiet and steam is no longer emerging from the Pressure Release, the float valve might be slightly stuck in its raised position. This happens to me all the time. Poke the float valve with a chopstick or a pen, and it'll return to its lowered position, allowing you to open the pot.

Q: Can I cook seafood in the Instant Pot?

A: Yes, but I wouldn't recommend cooking it under pressure. Most seafood is too delicate to turn out well when pressure cooked, and frankly, fishy smells are hard to get out of the silicone sealing ring. The Sauté setting is great for quick-cooking recipes, so if you'd rather use the Instant Pot than the stove top, you can make dishes like shrimp scampi in the uncovered pot the same way you would in a skillet.

Q: Can I cook in the Instant Pot without the inner pot inside?

A: No! Never put foods directly in the Instant Pot housing. Nothing's supposed to get in there. The inner pot must always be in place before anything goes into the Instant Pot. To be safe, wash, dry, and return the inner pot as soon as you finish cooking.

Q: Can I use the Instant Pot for canning?

A: Yes and no. You can use it as a hot-water bath, but *not* as a pressure canner. It doesn't create enough pressure to ensure safe results for low-acid or low-sugar foods that require pressure canning. I do use the Steam or Sterilize settings for canning jams, which saves a lot of time and water compared to a much larger water bath on the stove.

Q: What is this PIP cooking I keep hearing about?

A: You can cook cakes, breads, quiches, and many other dishes in a separate pan or heat-safe dish inside the Instant Pot, called pot-in-pot (PIP) cooking. The pan or dish sits on top of a trivet or raised steam rack placed on the bottom of the inner pot, which keeps the container above the water so the food can steam under pressure.

CHAPTER 1

Breakfast

LEMON–POPPY SEED BREAKFAST CAKE

This Bundt cake makes an indulgent breakfast treat or afternoon snack. The batter calls for tangy Greek yogurt, which keeps the cake moist and complements the lemon flavor. Drizzle the cake with the lemon glaze, dust it with confectioners' sugar, or leave it plain.

SERVES 8

3 large eggs

1 cup full-fat Greek yogurt

¾ cup granulated sugar

¼ cup poppy seeds

Finely grated zest of
1 lemon

4 tablespoons unsalted
butter, melted and cooled

1½ cups all-purpose flour

2 teaspoons baking powder

½ teaspoon kosher salt

GLAZE

1 tablespoon fresh
lemon juice

½ cup confectioners' sugar

Butter a 7-inch Bundt pan and dust with flour, tapping out the excess. Fold a 20-inch-long sheet of aluminum foil in half lengthwise twice to create a 3-inch-wide strip. Center it underneath the pan to act as a sling for lifting the pan in and out of the Instant Pot. Pour 1½ cups water into the pot and add the trivet.

In a bowl, whisk the eggs, then add the yogurt, granulated sugar, poppy seeds, lemon zest, and butter and whisk until smooth. In another bowl, whisk together the flour, baking powder, and salt. Gently stir the flour mixture into the egg mixture just until all of the flour is absorbed into the batter. Pour the batter into the prepared pan and spread in an even layer.

Holding the ends of the foil sling, lift the cake pan and lower it into the pot. Fold over the ends of the sling so they fit inside the pot. Secure the lid and set the Pressure Release to **Sealing**. Select the **Manual** or **Cake** setting and set the cooking time for 35 minutes at high pressure.

To make the glaze, in a bowl, stir together the lemon juice and confectioners' sugar until smooth.

When the timer goes off, let the pressure release naturally for 10 minutes, then move the Pressure Release to **Venting** to release any remaining steam. Open the pot, taking care not to drip condensation from the lid onto the cake. Wearing heat-resistant mitts, grasp the ends of the sling, lift the pan out of the pot, and place it on a cooling rack. Let the cake cool in the pan for 5 minutes, then invert the pan onto the rack, lift off the pan, and turn the cake right side up.

Let the cake cool for 20 minutes before drizzling the glaze over the top. Once glazed, let the cake cool to room temperature, then transfer to a serving plate. Cut into wedges and serve.

HARD-BOILED EGGS

1 cup water

Up to 12 large eggs, straight from the refrigerator

Hard-boiled eggs turn out perfectly every time when they're steamed under pressure in the Instant Pot. They're always evenly cooked, plus they are easier to peel than traditional boiled eggs. This recipe works if you are boiling only an egg or two or up to a dozen, and you can use either a quick release or a natural release. You can either put the eggs directly on the trivet, or use a wire-mesh, silicone, or metal steamer basket that fits inside the Instant Pot. Do not be tempted to use a solid bowl.

───────────────

NOTES For extra-large eggs, increase the cooking time to 7 minutes, and for jumbo eggs, increase the cooking time to 8 minutes.

You can also use the quick pressure release method for soft-boiled eggs. Cooking times for soft-boiled large, extra-large, and jumbo eggs are 3, 4, and 5 minutes, respectively.

5-Minute Quick Pressure Release Method: Pour the water into the Instant Pot and place a steamer basket or the trivet into the pot. Gently place up to 12 eggs into the basket or on top of the trivet, taking care not to crack the eggs as you add them. Secure the lid and set the Pressure Release to **Sealing**. Select the **Manual** setting and set the cooking time for 5 minutes at high pressure.

While the eggs are cooking, prepare an ice bath. When the timer goes off, let the pressure release naturally for 5 minutes, then move the Pressure Release to **Venting** to release the remaining steam. Open the pot and transfer the eggs to the ice bath to cool. Peel when ready to serve.

NOTE For extra-large eggs, increase the cooking time to 3 minutes, and for jumbo eggs, increase the cooking time to 4 minutes.

Natural Release Method: Pour the water into the Instant Pot and place a steamer basket or the trivet into the pot. Gently place up to 12 eggs into the basket or on top of the trivet, taking care not to crack the eggs as you add them. Secure the lid and set the Pressure Release to **Sealing**. Select the **Manual** setting and set the cooking time for 2 minutes at high pressure.

While the eggs are cooking, prepare an ice bath. When the timer goes off, let the pressure release naturally for 15 minutes, then move the Pressure Release to **Venting** to release any remaining steam. Open the pot and transfer the eggs to the ice bath to cool. Peel when ready to serve.

SAUSAGE AND GREEN ONION STRATA

A *strata* looks impressive, but it's actually easier to make than a skillet of scrambled eggs. It's also better because you get eggs, toast, and sausage all in one dish with a lot less attended cooking time. Mix the whole thing up and pop it into the fridge the night before for a make-ahead breakfast.

4 large eggs

1 cup low-sodium chicken broth (page 154)

½ teaspoon kosher salt

½ teaspoon freshly ground black pepper

4 green onions, white and green parts, sliced

4 cups cubed ciabatta

8 ounces fully cooked chicken sausage (2 or 3 links), halved lengthwise, then sliced crosswise ¼ inch thick

2 tablespoons chopped fresh flat-leaf parsley, for garnish

Lightly coat a 1½-quart soufflé dish or a 7-cup round heatproof glass container with olive oil or nonstick cooking spray.

In a bowl, whisk together the eggs, broth, salt, and pepper. Stir in the green onions, bread, and sausage, making sure all of the bread is coated with the egg mixture. Pour the mixture into the prepared dish, cover tightly with aluminum foil, and refrigerate overnight.

The next morning, fold a 20-inch-long sheet of aluminum foil in half lengthwise twice to create a 3-inch-wide strip. Center it underneath the still-covered soufflé dish to act as a sling for lifting the dish in and out of the Instant Pot. Pour 1½ cups water into the pot and add the trivet. Holding the ends of the foil sling, lift the dish and lower it into the pot. Fold over the ends of the sling so they fit inside the pot.

Secure the lid and set the Pressure Release to **Sealing**. Select the **Manual** setting and set the cooking time for 25 minutes at high pressure.

Let the pressure release naturally for at least 10 minutes, then move the Pressure Release to **Venting** to release any remaining steam. Open the pot and, wearing heat-resistant mitts, grasp the ends of the foil sling and lift the dish out of the pot. Uncover the dish, taking care to avoid getting burned from the steam.

Let the strata rest for 10 minutes before serving. Sprinkle the strata with the parsley, then slice and serve warm.

CRUSTLESS BROCCOLI AND CHEDDAR QUICHE

SERVES 4

6 large eggs

½ cup whole milk

½ teaspoon kosher salt

¼ teaspoon freshly ground black pepper

1 small head broccoli (about 8 ounces), finely chopped

3 green onions, white and green parts, sliced

1 cup shredded Cheddar cheese (4 ounces)

This quiche is satisfying as is, but you can add ½ cup chopped ham, crumbled bacon, or sausage for a meaty variation, if you like. The base—eggs, milk, salt, and pepper—works for nearly any filling you can think of.

Butter a 1½-quart soufflé dish or a 7-cup round heatproof glass container.

Fold a 20-inch-long sheet of aluminum foil in half lengthwise twice to create a 3-inch-wide strip. Center it underneath the soufflé dish to act as a sling for lifting the dish into and out of the Instant Pot. Pour 1½ cups water into the pot and add the trivet.

In a bowl, whisk together the eggs, milk, salt, and pepper. Stir in the broccoli, green onions, and cheese.

Pour the egg mixture into the prepared dish. Then, holding the ends of the foil sling, lift the dish and lower it into the Instant Pot. Fold over the ends of the sling so they fit inside the pot.

Secure the lid and set the Pressure Release to **Sealing**. Select **Manual** setting and set the cooking time for 25 minutes at high pressure.

Let the pressure release naturally for at least 10 minutes, then move the Pressure Release to **Venting** to release any remaining steam.

Open the pot and, wearing heat-resistant mitts, grasp the ends of the foil sling and lift the quiche out of the Instant Pot. Let the quiche cool for at least 5 minutes, giving it time to reabsorb any liquid and set up.

Slice and serve warm or at room temperature.

FLORENTINE OMELET

12 large eggs

½ cup milk or water

1 teaspoon kosher salt

½ teaspoon freshly ground black pepper

2 cups baby spinach

1 cup sliced cremini mushrooms

1 clove garlic, minced

¼ cup chopped oil-packed sun-dried tomatoes.

½ cup grated Parmesan cheese

2 tablespoons chopped fresh basil or flat-leaf parsley, for garnish (optional)

The Instant Pot and a 7-cup round heatproof glass container are your new best friends for omelets. What emerges from the pot is more like a steamed frittata, but you get the idea. This recipe is ideal for a busy morning when you don't have time to flip omelet after omelet in a pan on the stove top.

Lightly coat a 7-cup round heatproof glass container with butter or nonstick cooking spray.

Fold a 20-inch-long sheet of aluminum foil in half lengthwise twice to create a 3-inch-wide strip. Center it underneath the glass container to act as a sling for lifting the glass container into and out of the Instant Pot. Pour 2 cups water into the pot and place the trivet in the pot.

In a bowl, whisk together the eggs, milk, salt, and pepper until well blended, then stir in the spinach, mushrooms, garlic, tomatoes, and cheese.

Pour the egg mixture into the prepared glass container and cover tightly with aluminum foil. Then, holding the ends of the foil sling, lift the glass container and lower it into the Instant Pot. Fold over the ends of the sling so they fit inside the pot.

Secure the lid and set the Pressure Release to **Sealing**. Select the **Manual** setting and set the cooking time for 25 minutes at high pressure.

Let the pressure release naturally for at least 10 minutes, then move the Pressure Release to **Venting** to release any remaining steam. Open the pot and let the omelet sit for a minute or two, until it deflates and settles into its container. Then, wearing heat-resistant mitts, grasp the ends of the foil sling and lift the container out of the pot. Uncover the omelet, taking care to avoid getting burned from the steam.

Cut the omelet into wedges, sprinkle with the basil, and serve warm.

QUINOA PORRIDGE WITH PEPITAS AND HONEY

A topping of toasted *pepitas* (aka shelled pumpkin seeds) and a drizzle of honey add crunch and sweetness to this warming breakfast bowl, a nice alternative to oatmeal. Look for *pepitas* in the bulk foods section of well-stocked supermarkets and health food stores or order them online. If you can find only raw *pepitas*, toast them in a dry skillet over medium heat, stirring occasionally, for a few minutes, until they are aromatic and have taken on a little color.

SERVES 4

1 cup quinoa, rinsed and drained

2½ cups water

½ teaspoon kosher salt

½ cup almond milk

¼ cup roasted pepitas

¼ cup honey

Combine the quinoa, water, and salt in the Instant Pot. Secure the lid and set the Pressure Release to **Sealing**. Select the **Multigrain** setting and set the cooking time for 8 minutes at high pressure.

Let the pressure release naturally for at least 10 minutes, then move the Pressure Release to **Venting** to release any remaining steam. Open the pot and stir the porridge to incorporate any extra liquid.

Ladle the porridge into bowls and serve topped with the almond milk, pepitas, and honey, dividing them evenly.

BROWN BUTTER STEEL-CUT OATMEAL

SERVES 4 TO 6

2 tablespoons unsalted butter

1½ cups steel-cut oats

4½ cups water

½ teaspoon kosher salt

Brown sugar, for serving

Heavy cream, for serving

Steel-cut oats have a chewy, hearty texture, and I prefer them hands down to rolled oats. Once the pot comes up to pressure, they take just 12 minutes to cook on the Porridge setting. Taking the extra step of browning the oats in butter gives the oatmeal a toasty, rich flavor and helps to keep it from sticking to the pot. Once you have tried your hot breakfast cereal prepared this way, you'll never go back to plain oats and water.

———————————

Select **Sauté** on the Instant Pot and melt the butter. Add the oats and sauté, stirring often, for about 5 minutes, until aromatic and lightly toasted. Add the water and salt and stir to combine, making sure all of the oats are submerged in the liquid.

Secure the lid and set the Pressure Release to **Sealing**. Press the **Cancel** button to reset the cooking program, then select the **Porridge** setting and set the cooking time for 12 minutes at high pressure.

Let the pressure release naturally for at least 10 minutes, then move the Pressure Release to **Venting** to release any remaining steam. Open the pot and stir the oatmeal to incorporate any extra liquid.

Ladle the oatmeal into bowls and serve with brown sugar and cream.

VARIATIONS

Apple cinnamon: Stir in 1 apple, chopped, and ½ teaspoon cinnamon with the water.

Pumpkin spice: Stir in 1 cup pumpkin puree, ¼ cup maple syrup, and ¾ teaspoon pumpkin pie spice with the water.

Peanut butter–banana: Stir ¼ cup creamy peanut butter into the finished oatmeal. Top each serving with banana slices.

Blueberry almond/pecan: Top each serving with a handful of fresh blueberries, a scattering of toasted sliced almonds or pecans, and a drizzle of honey.

Savory sesame soy: Omit the salt. Stir in 2 tablespoons soy sauce and add ½ teaspoon toasted sesame oil with the water. Serve topped with a fried egg.

HONEY-TURMERIC TONIC

If you're feeling under the weather, a warm pot of this turmeric-tinted tonic is perfect for sipping all day long. Add a splash of coconut milk before serving to make it creamy, or leave it out for a lighter beverage. When I'm suffering from a head cold, I throw in a couple of Thai chiles for an extra hit of congestion-clearing spice.

———————————

Combine all of the ingredients in the Instant Pot. Stir to dissolve the honey.

Secure the lid and set the Pressure Release to **Sealing**. Select the **Soup/Broth** setting, adjust the pressure to Less, and set the cooking time to 5 minutes.

Let the pressure release naturally for 10 minutes, then move the Pressure Release to **Venting** to release any remaining steam. Open the pot and, using a slotted spoon, remove and discard the cinnamon sticks, turmeric and ginger slices, and chiles.

Ladle the tonic into mugs and serve, or re-cover and leave on the **Keep Warm** setting until you are ready to enjoy.

SERVES 4 TO 6

6 cups water

¼ cup honey

2 cinnamon sticks

2-inch knob fresh turmeric root, sliced ¼ inch thick

2-inch knob fresh ginger, sliced ¼ inch thick

2 Thai fresh or dried chiles, halved and seeded (optional)

CHAPTER 2

Beans
and
Grains

BASIC BEANS

MAKES 6 CUPS

**1 pound beans
(about 2¼ cups)**

**8 cups water, plus 6 cups
if you soak and drain the
beans before cooking**

2 teaspoons kosher salt

Whether or not you soak your beans, they'll cook much faster in the Instant Pot than on the stove top. Presoaked beans tend to finish up with fewer split skins, and some people contend they are easier to digest. But if you're short on time or haven't planned ahead, unsoaked beans will turn out just fine. The time charts on page 160 provide cooking times for a variety of beans, both soaked and unsoaked, and for unsoaked lentils. Just follow the basic instructions provided here, then set the cooking time according to the type of bean you are cooking. Cooked beans freeze well, so it's a good idea to cook more than you need so you can save some for another meal. Just spread the beans out on a sheet pan, let them cool to room temperature, and then transfer 2-cup portions to quart-size ziplock plastic freezer bags. They can be frozen for up to 6 months.

NOTES This recipe is easily halved. I often cook beans in 8-ounce batches (about 1⅛ cups) instead of cooking 1 pound. Be sure to halve the water and salt, as well. The cooking times remain the same.

If you like, you can add 1 tablespoon olive oil to the beans before cooking. The oil will help prevent the beans from foaming too much as they cook. For extra flavor, add a few garlic cloves, a bay leaf, and/or a diced onion before securing the lid.

To soak the beans, put them in the Instant Pot and add the 8 cups water and the salt. Leave the pot turned off and let the beans soak for 10 to 12 hours or up to overnight. You can then either drain the beans in a colander or not. If you drain them, they will be less flavorful because you have discarded the salt along with the water. Some people believe that discarding the soaking water makes the beans easier to digest, however. If you drain them, return them to the pot and add the 6 cups water.

If you decide to cook the beans without soaking them, put them in the Instant Pot and add the 8 cups water and the salt.

Secure the lid and set the Pressure Release to **Sealing**. Select the **Bean/Chili** setting and set the cooking time to the correct number of minutes at high pressure. (See the time chart on page 160.)

Let the pressure release naturally for 15 minutes, then move the Pressure Release to **Venting** to release any remaining steam. Wearing heat-resistant mitts, lift the inner pot out of the Instant Pot. You may either store the beans in their liquid in the refrigerator or drain them in a colander to freeze or use right away.

BORRACHO BEANS

There's no need to presoak the beans, which means you can make this dish any time a Tex-Mex craving arises. A simple pot of pinto beans is so good, and this is one of my favorite ways to make them. After all, how can you go wrong with beer and bacon? *Borracho* means "drunken" in Spanish and refers to the beer used in this pot of beans. It adds a distinctive flavor that I love, but if you'd rather not use beer, it's fine to increase the chicken or vegetable broth to 1½ cups for some sober frijoles.

_____

Select the **Sauté** setting on the Instant Pot and add the bacon. Sauté the bacon for 5 minutes, until it begins to render some fat but is not yet crispy. Add the onion, garlic, and chiles and sauté for about 5 minutes, until the onion has softened. Add the broth, beer, tomatoes and their liquid, pinto beans, salt, and water and stir well.

Secure the lid and set the Pressure Release to **Sealing**. Press the **Cancel** button to reset the cooking program, then select the **Bean/Chili** setting and set the cooking time for 50 minutes at high pressure.

Let the pressure release naturally (this will take about 35 minutes). Open the pot and stir in the cilantro.

Ladle the beans into small bowls (I like diner-style soup cups) and serve as a side dish.

VEGETARIAN VARIATION

Omit the bacon. Sauté the vegetables in 2 tablespoons olive oil in place of the bacon fat and use vegetable broth rather than chicken broth. Increase the salt to 2½ teaspoons and add 1 teaspoon smoked paprika along with the salt.

SERVES 6 TO 8

3 slices thick-cut bacon (about 4 ounces), diced

1 yellow onion, diced

2 cloves garlic, chopped

2 jalapeño chiles, seeded and diced

1 cup vegetable broth or low-sodium chicken broth (page 154)

½ cup Negra Modelo or other dark lager beer

1 (14½-ounce) can diced tomatoes and their liquid

1 pound (about 2½ cups) dried pinto beans

2 teaspoons kosher salt

4 cups water

¼ cup chopped fresh cilantro

CLASSIC HUMMUS

The secret to making a smooth, light, fluffy dip is to use warm just-cooked chickpeas. If serving as an appetizer, accompany with wedges of pita or a plate of crudités. It can also be spooned into a pita pocket along with tomato, cucumber, onion, and shredded lettuce for a hearty sandwich. The hummus will keep in an airtight container in the refrigerator for up to 5 days.

_____

If you decide to soak the beans, put them in the Instant Pot and add the 4 cups water and the salt. Leave the pot turned off and let the beans soak for 10 to 12 hours or up to overnight. You can then either drain the beans in a colander or not. If you drain them, return them to the pot and add the 3 cups water.

If you decide to cook the beans without soaking them, put them in the Instant Pot and add the 4 cups water and the salt.

When ready to cook the chickpeas, secure the lid and set the Pressure Release to **Sealing**. Select the **Bean/Chili** setting and set the cooking time for 25 minutes for soaked chickpeas or 40 minutes for unsoaked chickpeas.

Let the pressure release naturally for at least 15 minutes, then move the Pressure Release to **Venting** to release any remaining steam. At this point, you can leave the chickpeas in the pot on the **Keep Warm** setting for up to 10 hours.

When you are ready to make the hummus, open the pot. Ladle out ¾ cup of the cooking liquid and set it aside. Wearing heat-resistant mitts, lift the inner pot out of the Instant Pot and drain the chickpeas in a colander.

Transfer the drained chickpeas to a food processor or blender. Add the reserved ¾ cup cooking liquid, the tahini, lemon juice, garlic, cumin, and salt. Process at medium speed for about 1 minute, until the mixture is smooth and creamy.

If serving as an appetizer, spoon the hummus into the center of a wide, shallow serving bowl and spread it out in a thick circle. Sprinkle the parsley and paprika on top, then drizzle with the oil.

MAKES ABOUT 3½ CUPS

1 cup dried chickpeas

4 cups water, plus 3 cups if you soak and drain the beans

1 teaspoon kosher salt

HUMMUS

½ cup tahini

3 tablespoons fresh lemon juice (from 1 lemon)

2 cloves garlic, chopped

¼ teaspoon ground cumin

1 teaspoon kosher salt

TO SERVE (OPTIONAL)

1 tablespoon chopped fresh flat-leaf parsley

¼ teaspoon paprika

2 tablespoons extra-virgin olive oil

GREEK-STYLE GIGANTES BEANS WITH FETA

3 cups dried gigantes or other large white beans (see headnote)

8 cups water

1½ teaspoons kosher salt

¼ cup plus 2 tablespoons extra-virgin olive oil

1 clove garlic, peeled

1 large yellow onion, finely diced

1 celery stalk, finely diced

1 (28-ounce) can or (24-ounce) jar crushed tomatoes (about 3 cups)

1 teaspoon dried oregano

¼ teaspoon freshly ground black pepper

¼ cup chopped fresh flat-leaf parsley

½ cup crumbled feta cheese

NOTES If you prefer to drain your soaked beans before cooking them, return them to the pot with 6 cups fresh water.

To make this recipe vegan, omit the feta cheese.

Different varieties of large white beans are grown all over the world. If you cannot find the dried Greek *gigantes*, other types of large white beans will do, such as Corona, La Spagna, or large limas. Whether you prepare the traditional Greek bean or one of its cousins, you will end up with a warming and hearty dish. The beans are partially cooked and then simmered in an oregano-spiked tomato sauce and sprinkled with lots of feta cheese. Serve them with big hunks of crusty bread for sopping up all of the sauce.

Combine the beans, water, and salt in the Instant Pot. Leave the pot turned off and let the beans soak for 10 to 12 hours or up to overnight.

Secure the lid and set the Pressure Release to **Sealing**. Select the **Bean/Chili** setting and set the cooking time for 15 minutes at high pressure.

Let the pressure release naturally for 15 minutes, then move the Pressure Release to **Venting** to release any remaining steam. Open the pot, ladle out 1 cup of the cooking liquid, and set the liquid aside. Wearing heat-resistant mitts, lift the inner pot out of the Instant Pot and drain the beans in a colander. Return the now-empty inner pot to the Instant Pot housing.

Select the **Sauté** setting and heat the ¼ cup olive oil in the pot. Add the garlic, onion, and celery and sauté for about 5 minutes, until the onion has softened. Add the drained beans, the reserved 1 cup liquid, the tomatoes, oregano, and pepper and stir well.

Secure the lid and set the Pressure Release to **Sealing**. Press the **Cancel** button to reset the cooking program, then select the **Bean/Chili** setting and set the cooking time for 5 minutes at high pressure.

Let the pressure release naturally for at least 15 minutes, then move the Pressure Release to **Venting** to release any remaining steam.

Ladle the beans into a serving dish. Sprinkle the parsley and feta cheese over the beans, drizzle with the remaining 2 tablespoons olive oil, and serve.

VEGAN SLOPPY JOES

SERVES 8

¼ cup olive oil

1 yellow onion, diced

1 large bell pepper, seeded
and diced

1 large carrot, peeled
and diced

2 celery stalks, diced

3 cloves garlic, chopped

1 teaspoon kosher salt

½ teaspoon freshly ground
black pepper

1 tablespoon chili powder

½ teaspoon ground cumin

½ teaspoon smoked
paprika

¼ cup tomato paste

1 (15-ounce) can
tomato sauce

¼ cup firmly packed
brown sugar

2 tablespoons vegan
Worcestershire sauce
(see Notes)

1 tablespoon cider vinegar

4 cups vegetable broth

1 pound (2¼ cups) green
lentils, rinsed and drained

TO SERVE

8 hamburger buns, split
and toasted

Red onion slices

Pickle slices

These Sloppy Joes are made with protein-packed lentils instead of beef, which means just about anyone can enjoy them. Whether you're vegan, vegetarian, or just trying to incorporate more meatless meals into your dinner rotation, this is a dish for you.

———————————

Select the **Sauté** setting on the Instant Pot and heat the oil. Add the onion, bell pepper, carrot, celery, and garlic and sauté for about 10 minutes, until the onion is translucent but not yet beginning to brown. Add the salt, ground pepper, chili powder, cumin, paprika, and tomato paste and sauté for 1 minute. Add the tomato sauce, sugar, Worcestershire sauce, vinegar, broth, and lentils and stir well.

Secure the lid and set the Pressure Release to **Sealing**. Press the **Cancel** button to reset the cooking program, then select the **Bean/Chili** setting and set the cooking time for 25 minutes at high pressure.

Let the pressure release naturally for at least 10 minutes, then move the Pressure Release to **Venting** to release any remaining steam and open the pot.

Place the bun bottoms, cut side up, on individual plates and ladle the Sloppy Joe mixture onto the buns. Top with the onion and pickles, close with the bun tops, and serve hot.

NOTES Annie's Naturals makes a very good vegan (though not gluten-free) Worcestershire sauce. For a gluten-free alternative, substitute 2 tablespoons coconut aminos and ⅛ teaspoon ground cloves for the Worcestershire sauce.

To freeze any leftovers, ladle single-serving portions into the cups of a silicone muffin pan and slip into the freezer. When the portions have frozen solid, transfer them to ziplock plastic freezer bags and return to the freezer for up to 3 months.

BELUGA LENTIL SALAD WITH ITALIAN VINAIGRETTE

Beluga lentils are small, quick cooking, and hold their shape well, and their inky black color makes for an eye-catching dish. No soaking is required, and they cook perfectly with the pot-in-pot method. French green (aka Puy) lentils also hold their shape well, so you can substitute them here if you like. Marinate the lentils in the brightly flavored Italian vinaigrette while they're still warm, then stir in the crunchy vegetables for a satisfying salad.

―――――――――

In a 1½-quart stainless-steel bowl, stir together the lentils, 1½ cups of the water, and the salt.

Pour the remaining 2 cups water into the Instant Pot and place the trivet or a steamer basket in the pot. Put the bowl on the trivet or steamer basket. Select the **Manual** setting and set the cooking time for 20 minutes at high pressure.

While the lentils are cooking, make the vinaigrette. In a small bowl, whisk together the oil, vinegar, honey, garlic, oregano, and salt, mixing well.

When the lentils are ready, you can perform a quick release by moving the Pressure Release to **Venting** or you can let the pressure release naturally. Open the pot and, wearing heat-resistant mitts, remove the bowl of lentils from the Instant Pot.

Drain the lentils into a colander, then return them to the bowl. While they are still warm, pour half of the vinaigrette over the lentils and stir gently. Let cool for 20 minutes.

To finish the salad, in a serving bowl, toss together the lentils, carrot, celery, bell pepper, onion, and parsley. Taste and add more vinaigrette as needed. Serve the salad at room temperature or cover and chill for up to 2 days before serving.

SERVES 4 TO 6

1 cup beluga lentils

3½ cups water

½ teaspoon kosher salt

VINAIGRETTE

½ cup extra-virgin olive oil

¼ cup red wine vinegar

1 teaspoon honey, or 1½ teaspoons sugar

1 clove garlic, pressed or minced

1 teaspoon dried oregano

½ teaspoon kosher salt

SALAD

1 large carrot, peeled and diced

2 celery stalks, diced

1 red bell pepper, seeded and diced

½ small red onion, diced

¼ cup chopped fresh flat-leaf parsley

CHANA MASALA

If you like to prepare some of your weekday meals on the weekend, make this recipe and you'll be rewarded with a comforting Indian-inspired supper at the end of a busy day. Just make the Indian simmer sauce—it makes enough for three batches (and it's good for simmering other things too)—and soak your dried chickpeas ahead of time (if you're in a hurry, use canned chickpeas).

If using dried chickpeas, combine the chickpeas, 4 cups water, and salt in the Instant Pot. Leave the pot turned off and let the beans soak for 10 to 12 hours or up to overnight.

Secure the lid and set the Pressure Release to **Sealing**. Select the **Bean/Chili** setting and set the cooking time for 15 minutes at high pressure. Let the pressure release naturally for at least 15 minutes, then move the Pressure Release to **Venting** to release any remaining steam. Open the pot and, wearing heat-resistant mitts, lift the inner pot out of the Instant Pot and drain the chickpeas in a colander. Return the freshly cooked chickpeas to the inner pot and return to the Instant Pot housing. Press the **Cancel** button to reset the cooking program.

Add the simmer sauce and the remaining ¼ cup water and stir well (if using canned chickpeas, start here by adding them to the simmer sauce and ¼ cup water). Secure the lid and set the Pressure Release to **Sealing**. Select the **Bean/Chili** setting and set the cooking time for 3 minutes at high pressure.

When the timer goes off, you have three choices: you can perform a quick release by moving the Pressure Release to **Venting**; you can let the pressure release naturally for 15 minutes, then move the Pressure Release to **Venting** to release any remaining steam; or you can let the pressure release naturally, then leave the chickpeas in the pot on the **Keep Warm** setting for up to 10 hours.

Once you have opened the pot, stir in the lemon juice and cilantro. Spoon the chickpeas over the rice or accompany with naan on the side. Garnish with cilantro before serving.

SERVES 4

1 cup dried chickpeas, or 2 (15-ounce) cans chickpeas, rinsed and drained

4 cups water if using dried chickpeas, plus ¼ cup

1 teaspoon kosher salt

2 cups Indian simmer sauce, homemade (page 151) or store-bought

Juice of ½ lemon

2 tablespoons chopped fresh cilantro, plus coarsely torn leaves for garnish

Steamed rice or warmed naan, for serving

VARIATIONS

If you like, stir in 6 ounces baby spinach; 2 cups cubed paneer, winter squash, or potatoes; or 2 cups small cauliflower florets, frozen green peas, or mixed vegetables along with the cooked chickpeas. It's easy to add to this dish to make it a hearty one-pot meal.

BASIC RICE

Give it a rinse. I measure my rice into a wire-mesh strainer, then swish it around under running water to rinse off any extra starch. This step ensures that you won't end up with gummy, goopy rice, and the grains will come out separate and fluffy.

The shape of the pot is better suited to cooking larger batches of rice, so cook 1½ cups or more rice at a time. You can cook as much as 4 cups rice with consistent results.

Don't fill the pot more than half full. Grains and beans can foam and splatter when they cook. Keep the pot less than half full to prevent clogging the pressure valve.

Letting the rice rest on the Keep Warm setting for 10 minutes once it finishes cooking ensures that the rice cooks evenly, with no grains sticking or burning on the bottom of the pot.

Ever since I discovered how simple it is to make rice in the Instant Pot, I have never gone back to cooking it on the stove top. The method is straightforward, and there are no tricky ratios to remember: every type of rice can be cooked with a 1:1 ratio of rice to water. This ratio results in firm-textured, separate grains, so if you like your rice to have a softer consistency, use a bit more water. Whether you're cooking brown, white, long-grain, or short-grain rice, that ratio works perfectly. The Instant Pot does have one limitation when it comes to cooking rice, however: it's difficult to cook small amounts evenly, so I find it best to cook at least 1½ cups at a time; just freeze the extra rice for another meal. If you want to make a smaller amount, use the pot-in-pot method described on page 157.

Measure the rice into a wire-mesh strainer, then rinse under running water for 10 seconds, swishing it around. Drain well, which should take about 1 minute. Remove the inner pot from the Instant Pot and pour the rice and water into the inner pot. Jiggle the pot back and forth on the countertop so the rice settles in an even layer, then return the inner pot to the Instant Pot housing. Secure the lid and set the Pressure Release to **Sealing**.

For white rice, select the **Rice** setting. For brown rice, select the **Multigrain** setting and adjust the pressure to Less (20 minutes at high pressure). When the cooking program finishes, leave the Instant Pot on the **Keep Warm** setting for 10 minutes, then move the Pressure Release to **Venting** to release any remaining steam. Open the pot and, wearing heat-resistant mitts, lift the inner pot out of the Instant Pot housing. Use a rice paddle to scoop the rice out of the pot.

To Freeze: Line a sheet pan with parchment paper. Spread the hot rice in a thin layer on the pan, then let cool for 20 minutes, until room temperature. Scoop the cooled rice into small plastic bags in single or double portions and seal closed. Slip the bags into quart- or gallon-size ziplock plastic freezer bags, seal them closed, and freeze them flat. When you're ready to eat the rice, transfer it, still frozen, to a bowl, cover the bowl with plastic wrap, and heat in the microwave for 2 to 3 minutes, until piping hot.

JAMAICAN-STYLE RICE AND BEANS

When my husband and I first started dating, takeout from Back A Yard Caribbean Grill in Menlo Park, California, was a date-night standard. We'd bond over our favorite TV shows, our plates full of jerk chicken and salmon, stewed collard greens, and, my favorite side dish, rice and beans. Enjoy my easy Instant Pot version with Jamaican Jerk-Spiced Oxtails (page 103) or panfried salmon fillets for a fast weeknight dinner.

Combine all of the ingredients in the Instant Pot and stir to mix. Secure the lid and set the Pressure Release to **Sealing**. Select the **Multigrain** setting and set the cooking time for 22 minutes at high pressure.

Let the pressure release naturally for at least 10 minutes, then move the Pressure Release to **Venting** to release any remaining steam. Open the pot and scoop out and discard the garlic cloves, green onion, and chile.

Using a fork, stir and fluff the rice and beans, then serve hot.

NOTE If you want to use white basmati rice instead of brown, set the cooking time for 8 minutes.

SERVES 4 TO 6

1½ cups brown basmati rice

1 cup water

1⅓ cups cooked kidney beans (page 160), or 1 (15-ounce) can kidney beans, rinsed and drained

1 cup coconut milk

2 large cloves garlic, lightly smashed

1 green onion, lightly smashed

1 Scotch bonnet or habanero chile, left whole (optional)

½ teaspoon dried thyme

½ teaspoon freshly ground black pepper

1 teaspoon kosher salt

RISOTTO WITH LEMON AND PEAS

The Instant Pot is great for making risotto because much of the cooking time is unattended. It sure beats stirring a pot on the stove! I have called for Arborio rice here, but you can instead use Carnaroli, Vialone Nano, or other Italian risotto rice in its place. If you're looking for a vegan version, I have included a miso variation.

———————

Select the **Sauté** setting on the Instant Pot and heat the oil and butter. When the butter has melted, add the shallot and sauté for about 4 minutes, until softened and just beginning to brown. Stir in the rice and sauté for 1 minute.

Stir in the wine and lemon juice and sauté for about 2 minutes, just until the liquid has evaporated and the rice begins to sizzle in the pot. Stir in the broth, and, if using low-sodium broth, add the salt. Scrape down the sides of the pot to make sure all of the rice is submerged in the broth.

Secure the lid and set the Pressure Release to **Sealing**. Press the **Cancel** button to reset the cooking program, then select the **Manual** setting and set the cooking time for 5 minutes at high pressure.

Let the pressure release naturally for 10 minutes, then move the Pressure Release to **Venting** to release any remaining steam.

Open the pot and stir in the peas, Parmesan, pepper, and lemon zest. Serve immediately.

VARIATION

To make this a vegan risotto, use all olive oil instead of a mixture of oil and butter. Substitute sake for the white wine, vegetable broth for the chicken broth, and 2 tablespoons white miso paste for the Parmesan cheese.

SERVES 4 TO 6

2 tablespoons olive oil

2 tablespoons unsalted butter

1 large shallot, minced

1½ cups Arborio rice

⅓ cup dry white wine

Finely grated zest and juice of ½ large lemon

3 cups low-sodium chicken broth (page 154) or vegetable broth

¾ teaspoon kosher salt

1 cup fresh shelled or thawed frozen green peas

½ cup shredded Parmesan cheese

¼ teaspoon freshly ground black pepper

NOTE If you like your risotto to have a slightly looser texture, stir in an additional ¼ cup broth, warmed, just before serving.

BARLEY WITH MUSHROOMS AND SAGE

SERVES 6

2 tablespoons olive oil

2 large cloves garlic, finely chopped

8 ounces cremini mushrooms, sliced

1 teaspoon kosher salt

3 fresh sage leaves, finely chopped (about 1½ teaspoons)

1½ cups pearl barley

2 cups water or low-sodium chicken broth (page 154) or vegetable broth

1 tablespoon fresh lemon juice or rice vinegar

1 tablespoon soy sauce

NOTE To make this recipe gluten-free, substitute brown rice for the barley and tamari (double-check that the brand is gluten-free) for the soy sauce.

For a change of pace from the usual pot of rice or quinoa, make a savory side dish of barley flavored with mushrooms, soy sauce, garlic, and fresh sage. It pairs well with a wide variety of main dishes and sides. I especially like serving this alongside roasted chicken and buttered steamed brussels sprouts.

Select the **Sauté** setting on the Instant Pot and heat the oil. Add the garlic and sauté for about 1 minute, until it loses its raw smell and begins to turn golden. Add the mushrooms and salt and sauté for about 5 minutes, until the mushrooms have wilted and most of their liquid has evaporated. Stir in the sage and sauté for another minute or two, until you begin to see browned bits on the bottom of the pot. Add the barley, water, lemon juice, and soy sauce and stir to combine, scraping down the sides of the pot to make sure all of the barley is submerged in the cooking liquid.

Secure the lid and set the Pressure Release to **Sealing**. Press the **Cancel** button to reset the cooking program, then select the **Multigrain** setting and set the cooking time for 25 minutes at high pressure.

Let the pressure release naturally for at least 10 minutes, then move the Pressure Release to **Venting** to release any remaining steam. Open the pot and serve warm.

VARIATION

If you like, make a garnish of fried sage leaves. In a small frying pan over medium heat, warm 2 tablespoons olive oil. Add a small handful of small fresh sage leaves and fry, turning once, for about 2 minutes, until crisp. The leaves are done when they stop sizzling. Drain on a paper towel, sprinkle with salt, and use to garnish the finished dish.

CHAPTER 3

Soups
and
Chilis

CARROT-PARSNIP SOUP WITH GINGER

SERVES 4

2 tablespoons coconut oil

1 large yellow onion, diced

8 medium-to-large carrots (about 1 pound), peeled and sliced into ¼-inch-thick rounds

1 parsnip (about 8 ounces), peeled and sliced into ¼-inch-thick rounds

2-inch knob fresh ginger, peeled and diced

¾ teaspoon curry powder

4 cups vegetable broth

½ cup coconut milk

Kosher salt

Finely chopped fresh flat-leaf parsley, for serving (optional)

Spiced with pungent ginger and aromatic curry powder, this warming, comforting soup is enriched with just enough coconut milk to give it a silky, creamy texture. It is vegan, gluten-free, and dairy-free, which makes it a perfect first course or light lunch for a group with a variety of different dietary restrictions.

———————————

Select the **Sauté** setting on the Instant Pot and heat the coconut oil. Add the onion and sauté for about 5 minutes, until softened. Add the carrots, parsnip, ginger, curry powder, and broth and stir well.

Secure the lid and move the Pressure Release to **Sealing**. Press the **Cancel** button to reset the cooking program, then select the **Soup/Broth** setting and set the cooking time for 10 minutes at high pressure.

Perform a quick pressure release by moving the Pressure Release to **Venting**. Open the pot, add the coconut milk, and, using an immersion blender, puree until smooth. Taste and adjust with salt if needed.

Ladle the soup into bowls, sprinkle with the parsley, and serve right away.

TOMATO BASIL SOUP

2 tablespoons olive oil

1 small yellow onion, diced

2 carrots, peeled and diced

2 celery stalks, diced

½ teaspoon kosher salt

1 (28-ounce) can whole San Marzano tomatoes and their liquid

1½ cups low-sodium chicken broth (page 154) or vegetable broth

1 tablespoon tomato paste

1 slice rustic Italian bread or wheat bread (about 2 ounces), cut into ½-inch cubes

1 teaspoon dried basil

¼ teaspoon freshly ground black pepper

If you have homemade *soffritto* on hand, this recipe will go together more quickly (see Notes). If not, you'll need to start from scratch with chopped carrots, celery, and onions. Either way, it's fast enough for a weeknight and totally satisfying with crusty garlic bread or a grilled cheese sandwich served alongside.

───────────

Select the **Sauté** setting on the Instant Pot and heat the oil. Add the onion, carrots, celery, and salt and sauté for about 10 minutes, until the vegetables have softened and given up their liquid but are not browned. Add the tomatoes and their liquid, crushing the tomatoes with your hands as you add them to the pot. Add the broth, tomato paste, bread, basil, and pepper and stir well.

Secure the lid and set the Pressure Release to **Sealing**. Press the **Cancel** button to reset the cooking program, then select the **Soup/Broth** setting and set the cooking time for 5 minutes at high pressure.

Let the pressure release naturally for at least 10 minutes, then move the Pressure Release to **Venting** to release any remaining steam. Open the pot and use an immersion blender to puree the soup until smooth. Taste and adjust the seasoning with salt if needed.

Ladle the soup into bowls and serve piping hot.

NOTES If using already prepared *soffritto* (page 149), you will need 1 cup. Omit the oil, onion, carrots, celery, and salt. Combine the soffritto and all of the remaining ingredients in the Instant Pot, crushing the tomatoes with your hands as you add them to the pot. Secure the lid, select the **Soup/Broth** setting, and proceed as directed.

For a gluten-free soup, substitute a slice of gluten-free bread for the Italian bread or leave out the bread.

To make a creamy soup, add ¼ cup heavy cream just before pureeing the soup.

LEEK AND POTATO SOUP

Here is a simple, comforting soup for chilly days. This recipe makes a good-size batch. You can allow half of it to cool, then freeze it for up to 3 months, to have on hand for another easy cold-weather meal.

———————

Halve the leeks lengthwise, then thinly slice crosswise. Place the leeks in a large bowl and fill it with water. Swish the leeks around with your hands to dislodge any sandy soil. Let them sit in the water for a few minutes so the dirt settles on the bottom of the bowl. Using a slotted spoon, skim off the leeks from the top of the bowl and transfer them to a colander to drain.

Select the **Sauté** setting on the Instant Pot and melt the butter. Add the leeks, garlic, and salt and sauté for about 6 minutes, until the leeks are softened but not browned. Add the potatoes, broth, pepper, and bay leaf and stir well.

Secure the lid and set the Pressure Release to **Sealing**. Press the **Cancel** button to reset the cooking program, then select the **Soup/Broth** setting and set the cooking time for 5 minutes at high pressure.

Let the pressure release naturally for at least 15 minutes, then move the Pressure Release to **Venting** to release any remaining steam. Open the pot and remove and discard the bay leaf. Using an immersion blender, puree the soup until smooth. Blend in the lemon juice, then taste the soup and adjust with salt if needed.

Ladle the soup into bowls and serve piping hot.

NOTES If you like, make the recipe as directed through releasing the steam, then leave the soup in the pot on the Keep Warm setting for up to 10 hours. When you're ready to serve it, open the pot, remove and discard the bay leaf, and proceed as directed.

For a vegan soup, substitute olive oil for the butter.

SERVES 6 TO 8

1½ pounds leeks (about 4 medium), dark green ends discarded (trimmed to 6 inches)

2 tablespoons unsalted butter

2 cloves garlic, minced

½ teaspoon kosher salt

1½ pounds russet potatoes (about 2 large), peeled and sliced ⅛ inch thick

4 cups low-sodium chicken broth (page 154) or vegetable broth

¼ teaspoon freshly ground black pepper

1 bay leaf

1 tablespoon fresh lemon juice

RED LENTIL SOUP WITH SUMAC

I used to make this on the stove top all the time, but now I prefer to use the Instant Pot. Whip up a batch whenever you have a few minutes to spare, and it will stay piping hot until you're ready to enjoy it. The soup is brightly flavored from the squeeze of lemon juice stirred in at the end of cooking. That addition really makes the dish, so don't skip it! Serve the soup drizzled with extra-virgin olive oil and sprinkled with sumac (a lemony Middle Eastern spice) for a fresh, peppery finishing touch.

SERVES 4

1 tablespoon olive oil

2 carrots, peeled and diced

2 large celery stalks, diced

1 small yellow onion, diced

¼ teaspoon kosher salt

1 cup red lentils

4 cups water or vegetable broth

1 bay leaf

2 tablespoons fresh lemon juice

Extra virgin olive oil, for serving

Ground sumac, for serving

Select the **Sauté** setting on the Instant Pot and heat the olive oil. Add the carrots, celery, onion, and salt and sauté for about 5 minutes, until the onion has softened and is translucent. Add the lentils, water, and bay leaf and stir well.

Secure the lid and set the Pressure Release to **Sealing**. Press the **Cancel** button to reset the cooking program, then select the Select the **Soup/Broth** setting and set the cooking time for 15 minutes at high pressure.

Let the pressure release naturally for at least 10 minutes, then move the Pressure Release to **Venting** to release any remaining steam. Open the pot and stir in the lemon juice, then taste and adjust the seasoning with salt if needed.

Ladle the soup into bowls, top each serving with a drizzle of extra-virgin olive oil and a sprinkling of sumac, and serve right away.

NOTE If you like, add 1 teaspoon of a favorite spice blend to the soup when you add the lentils. Garam masala, *ras el hanout*, and *berbere* are three of my favorites.

MINESTRONE

SERVES 8

2 tablespoons olive oil

1 yellow onion, diced

1 carrot, peeled and diced

2 celery stalks, diced

½ teaspoon kosher salt

¼ teaspoon freshly ground
black pepper

¼ head green cabbage
(about 8 ounces), chopped

12 ounces zucchini
(2 medium), chopped

1 pound russet potatoes
(about 2 medium-large)
peeled and diced

1 (15-ounce) can cannellini
or kidney beans, rinsed
and drained

1 (15-ounce) can diced
tomatoes and their liquid

4 cups beef or
vegetable broth

1½ teaspoons Italian
seasoning

1 bay leaf

Grated Parmesan cheese,
for garnish

Chopped fresh flat-leaf
parsley, for garnish

Crusty Italian bread,
for serving

When I'm craving something hot and nutritious, a vegetable-filled bowl of minestrone hits the spot. This recipe doesn't include pasta, but it is easy to add some. Cook the pasta separately on the stove top, then stir it into the soup just before serving. Set out a basket of crusty bread slices along with the soup and you've got a hearty, satisfying meal. Use vegetable broth if you want to keep the soup vegetarian, and if you want it vegan as well, leave off the topping of Parmesan cheese.

Select the **Sauté** setting on the Instant Pot and heat the oil. Add the onion, carrot, celery, salt, and pepper and sauté for 5 minutes, until the onion has softened and is translucent. Add the cabbage, zucchini, potatoes, beans, tomatoes and their liquid, broth, Italian seasoning, and bay leaf and stir well. It's fine that the liquid doesn't cover all of the vegetables, as they will release their own liquid and sink down into the soup as it cooks.

Secure the lid and set the Pressure Release to **Sealing**. Press the **Cancel** button to reset the cooking program, then select the **Soup/Broth** setting and set the cooking time for 8 minutes at high pressure.

Let the pressure release naturally for at least 15 minutes, then move the Pressure Release to **Venting** to release any remaining steam. If you are not ready to serve the soup, you can leave the pot on the **Keep Warm** setting for up to 10 hours.

Open the pot and remove and discard the bay leaf. Ladle the soup into bowls, top with the cheese and parsley, and serve, accompanied with the bread.

CHICKEN AND DUMPLINGS

No matter how many times I make this dish, it seems like alchemy when the simple dough transforms into wonderfully light, tender dumplings. They're an adapted version of the classic-for-a-reason Feather Dumplings in *The Fannie Farmer Cookbook*, and they are my favorite drop-style dumplings.

Arrange the chicken breasts in a single layer in the Instant Pot and pour in 1 cup of the broth. Secure the lid and set the Pressure Release to **Sealing**. Select the **Poultry** setting and set the cooking time for 8 minutes at high pressure.

To make the dumpling dough, in a bowl, stir together the flour, bread crumbs, baking powder, salt, and pepper. Make a well in the center of the flour mixture and add the egg, milk, melted butter, shallot, and parsley. Using a fork, whisk together. Gradually mix the dry ingredients into the wet ingredients just until the flour is evenly absorbed. Cover the bowl and place it in the refrigerator.

When the cooking program ends, perform a quick release by moving the Pressure Release to **Venting**. Open the pot and, using tongs, transfer the chicken breasts to a carving board. Wearing heat-resistant mitts, lift the inner pot out of the Instant Pot housing and pour the cooking liquid into a large (4- to 8-cup) liquid measuring cup. Add the remaining 1 cup broth and the peas to the cooking liquid and reserve. Shred or slice the chicken into bite-size pieces.

Return the inner pot to the Instant Pot housing and press the **Cancel** button to reset the cooking program. Select the **Sauté** setting and melt the 2 tablespoons butter. Add the carrots, celery, onion, and salt and sauté for 5 minutes, until the onion has softened. Microwave the broth and peas for 3 minutes.

When the vegetables are ready, add the chicken, hot broth, and peas. Drop heaping tablespoonfuls of the dumpling dough into the pot, spacing evenly.

Cover the pot with a tempered glass lid and cook, covered, for 15 minutes. Remove the lid and, wearing heat-resistant mitts, lift the inner pot out of the Instant Pot housing. Ladle the dumplings, chicken, and broth into bowls and serve hot.

SERVES 4 TO 6

2 pounds boneless, skinless chicken breasts

2 cups low-sodium chicken broth (page 154)

1½ cups frozen green peas

2 tablespoons unsalted butter

3 large carrots, peeled and diced

2 celery stalks, diced

1 yellow onion, diced

1 teaspoon kosher salt

DUMPLINGS

1 cup all-purpose flour

½ cup fresh whole wheat bread crumbs

2 teaspoons baking powder

¾ teaspoon kosher salt

¼ teaspoon freshly ground black pepper

1 large egg

⅓ cup whole milk

2 tablespoons unsalted butter, melted

1 small shallot (about 1 ounce), minced

1½ tablespoons finely chopped fresh flat-leaf parsley

ITALIAN WEDDING SOUP

SERVES 4 TO 6

1 pound lean ground beef
(90 percent lean)

1 large egg

½ cup dried bread crumbs

2 cloves garlic, minced

1 tablespoon Italian
seasoning

½ teaspoon kosher salt

2 tablespoons olive oil

1 white or yellow
onion, diced

3 ounces pancetta, diced

6 ounces baby kale, or
1 bunch kale, stemmed
and chopped

1 (15-ounce) can cannellini
beans, rinsed and drained

4 cups low-sodium chicken
broth (page 154)

Grated Parmesan cheese,
for serving

A hot bowl of this hearty Italian American soup is one of my favorite meals for a chilly winter night. Garlicky, herbed meatballs, white beans, and kale make for a great combination of flavors and textures. It's a one-pot meal, especially with a loaf of artisanal bread served alongside.

———————————

In a bowl, combine the beef, egg, bread crumbs, garlic, Italian seasoning, and salt and mix with your hands until all of the ingredients are evenly distributed. Shape the mixture into meatballs 1 inch in diameter and set aside.

Select the **Sauté** setting on the Instant Pot and heat the oil. Add the onion and pancetta and sauté for about 5 minutes, until the onion has softened and is translucent. Add the kale and stir for about 2 minutes, until partially wilted. Add the meatballs, beans, and broth to the pot and stir gently to mix the meatballs and beans evenly into the broth.

Secure the lid and set the Pressure Release to **Sealing**. Press the **Cancel** button to reset the cooking program, then select the **Soup/Broth** setting and set the cooking time for 20 minutes at high pressure.

Let the pressure release naturally for at least 10 minutes, then move the Pressure Release to **Venting** to release any remaining steam.

Open the pot and ladle the soup into bowls. Serve hot, sprinkled with Parmesan.

TURKEY CHILE VERDE WITH PINTO BEANS

SERVES **6**

2 tablespoons olive oil

1 pound ground turkey (93 percent lean)

1 yellow onion, diced

2 poblano or Anaheim chiles, diced

2 jalapeño chiles, diced

2 serrano chiles, diced

3 cloves garlic, chopped

1 teaspoon kosher salt

1 teaspoon dried oregano

1 teaspoon ground cumin

¼ teaspoon cayenne pepper

2 (15-ounce) cans pinto beans, rinsed and drained, or 3 cups cooked pinto beans (page 160)

1 (12-ounce) jar Mexican-style salsa verde (tomatillo based)

½ cup low-sodium chicken broth (page 154)

¼ cup chopped fresh cilantro

Grated Monterey Jack cheese, for serving

Here's a lean, green chili that still packs some spicy heat! If you like yours mild, substitute a couple of seeded and chopped green bell peppers for the jalapeño and serrano chiles and omit the cayenne pepper. Serve this hearty stew with grated cheese on top and Cornbread (page 129), rice (page 40), or tortilla chips on the side.

Select the **Sauté** setting on the Instant Pot and heat the oil. Add the turkey and sauté, breaking it up with a wooden spoon or spatula as it cooks, for about 5 minutes, until cooked through and no traces of pink remain. Add the onion, chiles, garlic, salt, oregano, cumin, and cayenne and cook, stirring occasionally, for another 5 minutes, until the onion has softened and is translucent. Stir in the pinto beans, salsa verde, and broth.

Secure the lid and set the Pressure Release to **Sealing**. Press the **Cancel** button to reset the cooking program, then select the **Bean/Chili** setting and set the cooking time for 20 minutes at high pressure.

Let the pressure release naturally for at least 10 minutes, then move the Pressure Release to **Venting** to release any remaining steam. Open the pot and stir in the chopped cilantro.

Ladle into bowls and serve hot, topped with the cheese.

BEEF SHANK AND BARLEY SOUP

This soup has just the right balance of beef, barley, vegetables, and broth, making it hearty but not too thick and stewlike. Don't worry if the soup solidifies in the fridge overnight. It will thin out again nicely when reheated. If beef shank is not available, substitute any long-cooking cut of beef, and if you cannot find a parsnip, a rutabaga or turnip is a great stand-in.

_____

Season the beef shank on both sides with the salt and pepper. Select the **Sauté** setting on the Instant Pot and heat the oil. Using tongs, lower the beef shank into the pot and sear for 5 minutes on each side, until nicely browned. Transfer the shank to a plate.

Add the onion, parsnip, carrots, celery, mushrooms, and garlic and cook, stirring occasionally, for about 5 minutes, until the onion has softened and is translucent and the mushrooms are just beginning to wilt. Add the barley, tomato paste, bay leaf, broth, and water and stir well with a wooden spoon, using the spoon to nudge any browned bits from the pot bottom. Carefully lower the beef shank back into the pot.

Secure the lid and set the Pressure Release to **Sealing**. Press the **Cancel** button to reset the cooking program, then select the **Soup/Broth** setting and set the cooking time for 35 minutes at high pressure.

Let the pressure release naturally for at least 15 minutes, then move the Pressure Release to **Venting** to release any remaining steam.

Open the pot and, using the tongs, lift the shank out of the pot and transfer it to a plate or carving board. It may break up into pieces as you're lifting it, so lift slowly to avoid splashing. Chop the meat into small pieces and discard the bones. If you like, you can remove the gelatinous bits, though I enjoy their texture in the soup (and the collagen is good for you, too). Using a ladle or large spoon, skim the fat from the surface of the soup, then stir in the chopped beef.

At this point, you can leave the soup on the **Keep Warm** setting for up to 10 hours. To serve, ladle into bowls and serve piping hot.

SERVES **6**

1 crosscut beef shank, 1 to 1½ pounds

1 teaspoon kosher salt

½ teaspoon freshly ground black pepper

1 tablespoon avocado oil or other neutral oil with high smoke point

1 yellow onion, diced

1 parsnip, peeled and diced

2 large carrots, peeled and diced

2 celery stalks, diced

8 ounces cremini mushrooms, halved and sliced crosswise

2 cloves garlic, chopped

½ cup pearl barley

1 tablespoon tomato paste

1 bay leaf

4 cups beef or vegetable broth

3 cups water

SPICY BEEF AND BEAN CHILI

This isn't an authentic Texan-style chili—nor is it trying to be—but I do like this old-fashioned ground beef chili with plenty of tomatoes and beans, plus it goes together in a snap. If you think beans in chili is an abomination, just leave out the beans and double the amount of ground beef. I like mine topped with shredded cheese and green onions, but you can also add chopped fresh cilantro and sour cream.

———————————

Select the **Sauté** setting on the Instant Pot and heat the oil. Add the bell pepper, onion, celery, garlic, and salt and sauté for about 5 minutes, until the onion has softened and is translucent.

Add the beef and sauté, breaking it up with a wooden spoon or spatula as it cooks, for about 5 minutes, until cooked through and no traces of pink remain. Stir in the chili powder, oregano, cayenne pepper if using, and tomato paste until the tomato paste is evenly mixed, then add the tomatoes and their liquid, the beans, and water, and stir to combine.

Secure the lid and set the Pressure Release to **Sealing**. Press the **Cancel** button to reset the cooking program, then select the **Manual** setting and set the cooking time for 20 minutes at high pressure. (If you plan to serve the chili with rice, put the rice on to cook at this point.)

When the timer goes off, you can perform a quick release by moving the Pressure Release to **Venting**, or you can let the pressure release naturally for 20 minutes, then move the Pressure Release to **Venting** to release any remaining steam.

Serve the chili in bowls topped with the cheese and green onions, either over rice or with cornbread on the side.

SERVES 8 TO 10

¼ cup avocado oil or other neutral oil with high smoke point

2 green bell peppers, seeded and chopped

1 large yellow onion, chopped

4 celery stalks, chopped

4 cloves garlic, chopped

2 teaspoons kosher salt

2 pounds lean ground beef (90 percent lean)

¼ cup chili powder

1½ teaspoons dried oregano

¼ teaspoon cayenne pepper (optional)

¼ cup tomato paste

2 (14-ounce) cans diced tomatoes and their liquid

2 (15-ounce) cans kidney beans, rinsed and drained

½ cup water

1½ cups mixed shredded cheese, such as Cheddar, Monterey Jack, and/or Colby (6 ounces)

3 green onions, white and green parts, sliced thinly

Steamed rice (page 40) or Cornbread (page 129), for serving

CHAPTER 4

Poultry

ARROZ CON POLLO

SERVES 4 TO 6

SOFRITO

1 large yellow onion,
cut into 1-inch pieces

1 red bell pepper, seeded
and cut into 1-inch pieces

8 cloves garlic

1 large bunch cilantro
(3 ounces), leaves and stems

¼ cup pimiento-stuffed
green olives

1 tablespoon capers, rinsed
and drained

2 teaspoons kosher salt

1 teaspoon freshly ground
black pepper

1 teaspoon dried oregano

½ cup olive oil

ARROZ CON POLLO

1 tablespoon olive oil

¼ cup pimiento-stuffed
green olives, sliced

1 tablespoon capers, rinsed
and drained

1½ pounds boneless,
skinless chicken thighs,
cut into 1-inch pieces

1½ cups long-grain
white rice

1 cup low-sodium chicken
broth (page 154)

1 cup tomato sauce

¼ cup chopped fresh
cilantro, for serving

This is a quick version of Puerto Rican–style *arroz con pollo*. I'm not claiming that it's authentic, but it is delicious! The recipe starts with *sofrito*, the base of many Puerto Rican dishes. It's a blend of peppers, onions, and spices, and it comes together quickly in a food processor or blender. You'll end up with enough *sofrito* for about eight batches of *arroz con pollo*; just freeze it in ½-cup portions (I like to use a muffin pan lined with silicone muffin cups for this), and it will keep for about 4 months.

To make the sofrito, combine all of the ingredients in a food processor or blender and process until a thick paste forms. Measure ½ cup for this recipe, then store the remainder in ½-cup portions in ziplock plastic freezer bags (see headnote).

Select the **Sauté** setting on the Instant Pot and heat the 1 tablespoon oil. Add the ½ cup sofrito and sauté for 5 minutes, until it loses its raw onion bite. Add the olives, capers, and chicken pieces and stir to combine, coating the chicken evenly. Add the rice, pouring it in an even layer over the chicken.

In a 4-cup liquid measuring cup or in a bowl, stir together the broth and tomato sauce. Pour this mixture over the rice, making sure all of the grains are coated with the liquid. Use a spoon to scrape down any rice grains from the sides of the pot.

Secure the lid and set the Pressure Release to **Sealing**. Press the **Cancel** button to reset the cooking program, then select the **Poultry** setting and set the cooking time for 10 minutes at high pressure.

Let the pressure release naturally for 10 minutes, then move the Pressure Release to **Venting** to release any remaining pressure.

Open the pot, then use a big serving spoon to scoop down to the bottom of the pot to dish out servings of the rice and chicken together. Top with the cilantro and serve immediately.

PLUM CHILI CHICKEN

For our first Valentine's Day dinner, I made this dish for my husband, a favorite from his childhood. This is my Instant Pot makeover of that classic *Better Homes & Gardens* recipe, which appeared in its now out-of-print cookbook *100 Best Chicken Recipes*. The sweet and spicy sauce is made with plum jam, but if you cannot track down a jar, you can use apricot jam. Serve the chicken with steamed rice and broccoli for an easy weeknight dinner.

_____

In a small bowl, whisk together the jam, water, soy sauce, sambal oelek, ginger, green onions, and garlic.

Place the chicken pieces in the Instant Pot and pour the sauce mixture over them. Using tongs, move the chicken pieces around to coat them evenly with the sauce, then arrange them in a single layer.

Secure the lid and set the Pressure Release to **Sealing**. Select the **Poultry** setting and set the cooking time for 8 minutes at high pressure.

Let the pressure release naturally for at least 10 minutes, then move the Pressure Release to **Venting** to release any remaining steam. Open the pot and transfer the cooked chicken to a serving dish, working carefully to keep the pieces whole.

Press the **Cancel** button to reset the cooking program, then select the **Sauté** setting. Let the sauce simmer for about 8 minutes, until it has thickened into a glaze. Spoon the glaze over the chicken and serve hot.

NOTES If you prefer to use bone-in, skin-on chicken, sear the pieces first in 1 tablespoon of avocado oil or other neutral oil with high smoke point on the **Sauté** setting for 3 minutes per side, then add the sauce and turn to coat the pieces evenly. Secure the lid, set the Pressure Release to **Sealing**, press the **Cancel** button to reset the cooking program, then select the **Poultry** setting and proceed as directed, increasing the cooking time to 10 minutes.

This recipe contains just enough liquid to come up to pressure in the 5- and 6-quart models of the Instant Pot. If you are making it in the DUO80 model, double the amount of water (or the whole recipe). It may take a few more minutes to reduce the sauce.

SERVES 3 TO 4

½ cup plum jam

½ cup water

2 tablespoons soy sauce

1 tablespoon sambal oelek

¼ teaspoon ground ginger

1 bunch green onions (about 4 ounces), thinly sliced

1 clove garlic, chopped

1½ to 2 pounds boneless, skinless chicken thighs or breasts

CAJUN CHICKEN AND SAUSAGE JAMBALAYA

SERVES 4

1 tablespoon avocado oil or other neutral oil with high smoke point

6 ounces andouille sausage (2 links), sliced

1 yellow onion, chopped

3 cloves garlic, chopped

1 cup long-grain white rice

1 bay leaf

½ teaspoon dried oregano

¼ teaspoon freshly ground white pepper

¼ teaspoon freshly ground black pepper

⅛ teaspoon cayenne pepper

1½ cups low-sodium chicken broth (page 154)

1 tablespoon Worcestershire sauce

1 pound boneless, skinless chicken thighs (4 thighs), cut into 1-inch pieces

A filling one-pot rice dish with chunks of chicken thigh and slices of spicy andouille sausage, jambalaya is one of my husband's favorite dishes. It's easy to throw together for dinner, and I'm happy to make it often, especially when we're tired of the usual soups and stews. If you like, add seeded and chopped bell pepper and/or celery with the onion. A bottle of hot sauce on the table is mandatory. Frank's RedHot is my pairing of choice.

———————————

Select the **Sauté** setting on the Instant Pot and heat the oil. Add the sausage and cook, stirring occasionally, for about 5 minutes, until lightly browned. Add the onion and garlic and sauté for about 3 minutes, until slightly softened. Add the rice, bay leaf, and spices and sauté, stirring often, for 1 minute longer.

Add the broth, Worcestershire sauce, and chicken and stir to combine, scraping down the sides of the pot to make sure all of the rice is covered with the cooking liquid.

Secure the lid and set the pressure release to **Sealing**. Press the **Cancel** button to reset the cooking program, then select the **Poultry** setting and set the cooking time for 10 minutes at high pressure.

Let the pressure release naturally for at least 10 minutes, then move the Pressure Release to **Venting** to release any remaining steam. Open the pot and serve the jambalaya immediately.

DIJON CHICKEN AND WILD RICE PILAF

SERVES 2 TO 3

PILAF

1 cup wild rice pilaf blend
(see Note)

1 cup water

¼ teaspoon kosher salt

1 tablespoon unsalted butter

CHICKEN

½ cup low-sodium chicken
broth (page 154)

¼ cup dry sherry

2 tablespoons Dijon mustard

2 cloves garlic, chopped

1 teaspoon dried thyme

½ teaspoon kosher salt

½ teaspoon freshly ground
black pepper

1 tablespoon unsalted
butter or olive oil

1 yellow onion, sliced

1½ to 2 pounds bone-in
chicken drumsticks or
boneless, skinless thighs
or breasts

NOTE Choose a wild rice
pilaf blend that is mostly
made up of either white
rice or quick cooking brown
rice (I like the Basmati Rice
Blend from Trader Joe's).
Regular brown rice and
wild rice take much longer
to cook than the chicken.

This recipe takes advantage of the pot-in-pot (aka PIP) cooking technique, described in detail on page 157. Chicken simmers in a French-inspired mustard sauce in the inner pot while the rice pilaf cooks in a bowl on top of a raised steam rack.

To make the pilaf, in a 1½-quart stainless-steel bowl, stir together the rice, water, and salt. Top with the butter. Set aside.

To make the chicken, in a small bowl or liquid measuring cup, whisk together the broth, sherry, mustard, garlic, thyme, salt, and pepper.

Select the **Sauté** setting on the Instant Pot and melt the butter. Add the onion and sauté for 5 minutes, until softened and translucent. Using tongs, nestle the chicken pieces in the onion, then pour the broth-mustard mixture over the chicken.

Place a tall steam rack in the pot, making sure all of its legs are resting firmly on the bottom. Place the bowl of rice on the rack. Secure the lid and set the Pressure Release to **Sealing**. Press the **Cancel** button to reset the cooking program, then select the **Manual** setting and set the cooking time for 8 minutes at high pressure.

Let the pressure release naturally for at least 10 minutes, then move the Pressure Release to **Venting** to release any remaining steam. Alternatively, let all of the pressure release naturally.

Open the pot and, wearing heat-resistant mitts, remove the bowl of rice and the rack, then fluff the rice with a fork before serving. You can serve the chicken and sauce as they are, transferring them to a serving dish, or you can reduce and thicken the sauce before serving, which I prefer. To reduce the sauce, transfer the chicken to a serving plate, press the **Cancel** button to reset the cooking program, then select the **Sauté** setting and reduce the sauce for 7 minutes. Again, wearing mitts, lift out the inner pot and pour the sauce over the chicken.

Serve the chicken and sauce right away, with the pilaf on the side.

CHICKEN CACCIATORE

This version of an old-fashioned Italian favorite calls for a lot less liquid than is customary, but you still end up with a generous amount of flavorful sauce, thanks to the ability of the Instant Pot to retain moisture. Use bone-in chicken for the best flavor, or use boneless, skinless chicken thighs for a faster variation (see Note). Serve the chicken with crusty Italian bread, pasta, or rice for sopping up the sauce.

―――――――――

Season the chicken thighs on both sides with the salt and pepper.

Select the **Sauté** setting on the Instant Pot and heat the oil. Add half of the thighs, skin side down, and sear for 4 minutes, until browned. Transfer the seared chicken to a plate. Repeat with the remaining thighs.

Add the bell pepper, onion, and garlic to the pot and sauté for 3 minutes, just until the onions have softened slightly. Add the tomatoes and their liquid, wine, broth, tomato paste, Italian seasoning, red pepper flakes, and bay leaf and stir well with a wooden spoon, nudging any browned bits from the pot bottom. Return the chicken to the pot and, using tongs, turn each piece to coat it with the cooking liquid, then nestle the pieces in a single layer in the liquid.

Secure the lid and set the Pressure Release to **Sealing**. Press the **Cancel** button to reset the cooking program, then select the **Poultry** setting and set the cooking time for 12 minutes at high pressure.

Perform a quick release by moving the Pressure Release to **Venting**, or let the pressure release naturally.

Open the pot. You can serve the chicken and sauce as they are, transferring them to a serving dish, or you can reduce the sauce to make it thicker and richer before serving. To reduce the sauce, using a slotted spoon, transfer the chicken, bell pepper, and onion to a serving dish, press the **Cancel** button to reset the cooking program once more, then select the **Sauté** setting and reduce the sauce for 10 to 12 minutes. Spoon the sauce over the chicken and vegetables and serve right away.

SERVES 4 TO 6

3 pounds bone-in, skin-on chicken thighs (about 8 thighs)

1 teaspoon kosher salt

½ teaspoon freshly ground black pepper

1 tablespoon olive oil

1 large red bell pepper, seeded and sliced lengthwise into strips

1 yellow onion, sliced

3 cloves garlic, chopped

1 (15-ounce) can diced tomatoes and their liquid

½ cup dry red wine

¼ cup low-sodium chicken broth (page 154) or water

2 tablespoons tomato paste

1½ teaspoons Italian seasoning

½ teaspoon red pepper flakes (optional)

1 bay leaf

NOTE To make this recipe with boneless, skinless chicken thighs, skip the searing step.

POMEGRANATE WALNUT CHICKEN

Here is a simplified take on *fesenjān*, a classic Iranian dish of chicken simmered in a rich, tangy sauce of toasted walnuts and pomegranate molasses. You can either cut up a whole chicken or use an equivalent weight of bone-in, skin-on drumsticks and thighs. (For a faster version, see the Notes for instructions on how to use boneless chicken pieces.) Easy but elegant, this dish is great for both weeknight suppers and weekend dinner parties.

———————

In a food processor, pulse the walnuts until finely and evenly ground. Season the chicken pieces on both sides with the salt and pepper.

Select the **Sauté** setting on the Instant Pot and heat the oil. Add half of the chicken pieces and sear, turning once, for 4 minutes on each side, until browned. Transfer the seared chicken to a plate. Repeat with the remaining chicken.

Add the ground walnuts to the oil and rendered chicken fat remaining in the Instant Pot and sauté for 3 minutes. They will become a bit toasty and aromatic, leaving lots of browned bits stuck to the bottom of the pot. Stir in the onion and garlic and sauté for 3 minutes, until the onion is slightly softened. Stir in the cinnamon and sauté for 1 more minute.

Stir in the pomegranate molasses and water, using a wooden spoon to nudge all of the browned bits from the pot bottom and incorporate them into the sauce. Return the chicken pieces to the pot, coating them with the sauce and arranging the pieces in a single layer. Secure the lid and set the Pressure Release to **Sealing**. Press the **Cancel** button to reset the cooking program, then select the **Poultry** setting and set the cooking time for 10 minutes at high pressure.

Let the pressure release naturally for at least 10 minutes, then move the Pressure Release to **Venting** to release any remaining steam. Open the pot and use a ladle or large spoon to skim off the fat from the surface of the sauce.

To serve, using a slotted spoon, arrange the chicken over the rice on individual plates and then ladle the sauce on top. Sprinkle each serving with pomegranate seeds and parsley.

SERVES 4 TO 6

1½ cups walnut halves and pieces

3 to 3½ pounds bone-in, skin-on chicken pieces (breasts, thighs, and drumsticks)

1½ teaspoons kosher salt

½ teaspoon freshly ground black pepper

1 tablespoon olive oil

1 yellow onion, diced

1 clove garlic, chopped

½ teaspoon ground cinnamon

⅔ cup pomegranate molasses

⅔ cup water

Steamed long-grain white rice, for serving (see Notes)

½ cup pomegranate seeds

¼ cup chopped fresh flat-leaf parsley

NOTES Start a pot of rice on the stove top right after selecting the Poultry setting. It will be ready when the chicken is done.

To make this recipe with boneless, skinless chicken breasts or thighs, skip the searing step and use the oil to sauté the walnuts. Omit defatting the sauce before serving.

WHOLE CHICKEN WITH MUSHROOM SAUCE

SERVES 4

1 (3½- to 4-pound) chicken

2 teaspoons kosher salt

½ teaspoon freshly ground
black pepper

1 teaspoon sweet paprika

2 tablespoons avocado oil
or other neutral oil with
high smoke point

1 yellow onion, sliced

8 ounces cremini
mushrooms, sliced

1 clove garlic, chopped

1 tablespoon tomato paste

½ teaspoon dried thyme

½ teaspoon dried oregano

1 cup low-sodium chicken
broth (page 154)

2 tablespoons all-purpose
flour

Yes, it's true. You can cook a whole chicken in the Instant Pot. Just keep in mind a couple of things: the chicken must weigh 4 pounds or less (aka a broiler-fryer), and it won't come out with a crispy, crackling skin like it would from the oven. I find that the convenience and the speed of the Instant Pot make up for those two differences, as does the delicious mushroom sauce. This recipe yields lots of extra sauce, great for spooning on mashed potatoes.

———————————

Pat the chicken dry with paper towels. Tuck the wings tips under, so they sit flat against the chicken, tie the drumsticks together with kitchen string, then season the chicken all over with the salt, pepper, and paprika.

Select the **Sauté** setting on the Instant Pot and heat the oil for 2 minutes. Swirl the oil around to make sure it coats the center of the pot. Using tongs, lower the chicken, back side down, into the pot and sear for 5 minutes, until browned. Some of the chicken skin may stick to the pot bottom, and that's fine. This happens to me about half the time, which is why I sear it on the back side first. The sticking helps to form a protective layer on the pot so the skin on the breast side stays intact. Flip the chicken onto its breast side and sear it for 5 more minutes, until browned. Transfer it to a plate and set it aside.

Add the onion, mushrooms, and garlic to the pot and sauté for about 5 minutes, until the onion has softened and the mushrooms have wilted and given up some of their liquid. Stir in the tomato paste, thyme, and oregano and sauté for 2 more minutes to blend the flavors. Add the broth and stir well with a wooden spoon, nudging any browned bits from the pot bottom.

Place the trivet in the Instant Pot on top of the onions and mushrooms. Using the tongs, carefully lower the chicken, breast side up, onto the trivet. Secure the lid and set the Pressure Release to **Sealing**. Press the **Cancel** button to reset the cooking program, then select the **Poultry** setting and set the cooking time for 20 minutes at high pressure.

CONTINUED

Perform a quick release by moving the Pressure Release to **Venting**. Open the pot and, wearing heat-resistant mitts, grab the arms of the trivet and lift the trivet with the chicken out of the pot. Transfer the chicken to a carving board to rest while you finish making the sauce.

Still wearing the mitts, lift the inner pot out of the Instant Pot and strain the cooking liquid into a fat separator. Set the mushrooms and onions aside. If you don't have a fat separator, strain the liquid through a fine-mesh strainer placed over a bowl and scoop off the fat from the surface with a ladle or large spoon. Pour the cooking liquid back into the inner pot and discard the fat.

Add the flour to the inner pot and, using an immersion blender, blend the flour into the cooking liquid, tilting the pot so the head of the blender is fully submerged in the liquid, until no lumps remain. Stir the onions and mushrooms into the blended sauce.

Return the inner pot to the Instant Pot housing. Press the **Cancel** button to reset the cooking program, then select the **Sauté** setting. Let the sauce come to a boil and then cook for about 1 minute, or until thickened. Immediately press the **Cancel** button to turn off the Instant Pot so the sauce does not overcook. Taste and adjust the seasoning with salt if needed.

Carve the chicken and arrange on a platter. Spoon the mushroom sauce over the top and serve immediately.

NOTES If you want to use a frozen chicken, thaw it fully before you try this method. People regularly ask me if they can cook a whole frozen chicken in the Instant Pot, and I always tell them they should plan on something else for dinner that night. They need to put the frozen bird in the fridge to defrost and then try this recipe in a day or two when the chicken is no longer frozen solid.

If you are using a brined chicken, you may want to use less salt (or none if you're sensitive to sodium) when seasoning the chicken.

THANKSGIVING TURKEY BREAST AND GRAVY

For a small-scale Thanksgiving dinner (or an easy turkey dinner anytime), cook a split turkey breast in the Instant Pot. It's easier and faster than roasting a whole bird in the oven and making gravy on the stove top. This method works with turkey wings, thighs, or drumsticks. Just increase the cooking time by 5 minutes for dark meat, and don't overload the pot (no more than 4 pounds).

———————

Pat the turkey breast dry with paper towels, then season on both sides with the salt, pepper, and paprika. Put the Instant Pot trivet on a plate.

Select the **Sauté** setting on the Instant Pot and heat the oil. Place the turkey breast, skin side down, in the pot and sear for 5 minutes, until well browned. Using the tongs, transfer the turkey breast, skin side up, to the trivet.

Add the onions and garlic to the pot and sauté for 5 minutes, until the onions have softened. Add the poultry seasoning and broth and stir, nudging any browned bits from the pot bottom. Wearing heat-resistant mitts, lower the trivet with the turkey breast into the Instant Pot, resting it on top of the onions. Secure the lid and set the Pressure Release to **Sealing**. Press the **Cancel** button to reset the cooking program, then select the **Poultry** setting and set the cooking time for 25 minutes at high pressure.

Perform a quick release by moving the Pressure Release to **Venting**. Open the pot and insert an instant-read thermometer into the center of the breast away from the bone. The thermometer should register at least 160°F (if lower than 160°F, cook the turkey on the **Manual** setting for a few more minutes). Wearing the heat-resistant mitts, lift the trivet with the turkey breast out of the pot. Transfer the turkey breast to a carving board and tent it with aluminum foil.

Sprinkle the flour into the pot, then use an immersion blender to blend the onion mixture until smooth. Press the **Cancel** button to reset the cooking program, select the **Sauté** setting, and simmer the gravy for 1 to 2 minutes, until thickened. Press the **Cancel** button, and season with salt and pepper if needed. Carve the turkey, arrange on a platter, and serve with the gravy.

SERVES 4

1 bone-in, skin-on split turkey breast, 2½ to 3½ pounds

1½ teaspoons kosher salt

½ teaspoon freshly ground black pepper

1 teaspoon sweet paprika

1 tablespoon avocado oil or other neutral oil with high smoke point

2 yellow onions, chopped

4 cloves garlic

1 teaspoon poultry seasoning

2 cups low-sodium chicken broth (page 154) or turkey broth

2 tablespoons all-purpose flour

MOMO MEATBALLS WITH CILANTRO CHUTNEY

This is one of my favorite recipes, inspired by a mind-blowingly delicious meal of *momos* (aka Nepalese pot stickers) I enjoyed one year at the Outside Lands festival in San Francisco. Folding beautiful dumplings is time-consuming and takes a lot of experience, however, so I've instead taken the basic flavors and infused them into turkey meatballs, adding rice to the ground meat for a one-pot meal—less work, similar flavors, and totally satisfying. I like them on their own, on top of zucchini noodles, or served with cauliflower rice on the side.

To make the sauce, select the **Sauté** setting on the Instant Pot and heat the oil. Add the onion and sauté for 10 minutes, until softened and beginning to brown. Add the tomatoes and water, stir to mix well, and bring to a simmer.

To make the meatballs, in a bowl, combine the turkey, rice, ras el hanout, and salt and mix with your hands until all of the ingredients are evenly distributed. Don't worry about overmixing, as you want the rice and spices to be evenly incorporated into the meat. When everything is well combined, shape the mixture into 12 meatballs each slightly larger than a golf ball.

Place the meatballs in a single layer in the simmering sauce and spoon a little of the sauce over the top of each one. Secure the lid and set the Pressure Release to **Sealing**. Press the **Cancel** button to reset the cooking program, then select the **Poultry** setting and set the cooking time for 15 minutes at high pressure.

While the meatballs are cooking, make the chutney. In a mini chopper or in a mortar with a pestle, combine all of the chutney ingredients and process or grind into a rough paste.

When the timer goes off, you can perform a quick release by moving the Pressure Release to **Venting**, or you can let the pressure release naturally and leave the meatballs on the **Keep Warm** setting for up to 10 hours.

Serve the meatballs in their sauce with a spoonful of chutney on top of each.

**SERVES 3 TO 4
(MAKES 12 MEATBALLS)**

SAUCE

2 tablespoons avocado oil or other neutral oil with high smoke point

1 yellow onion, chopped

1 (28-ounce) can or (24-ounce) jar crushed tomatoes (about 3 cups)

½ cup water

MEATBALLS

1 pound ground turkey (93 percent lean)

½ cup long-grain white rice or quick-cooking brown rice

1 teaspoon ras el hanout spice blend

1 teaspoon kosher salt

CHUTNEY

1 bunch cilantro (2 ounces), leaves and stems

1 tablespoon fresh lemon juice

1 teaspoon toasted sesame oil

¼ teaspoon cayenne pepper

1 large green onion, white and green parts cut into ½-inch lengths

½ teaspoon kosher salt

¼ teaspoon freshly ground black pepper

CHAPTER 5

Beef
and
Pork

FETTUCCINE WITH BOLOGNESE SAUCE

SERVES 8 (MAKES
ABOUT 10 CUPS SAUCE)

BOLOGNESE SAUCE

2 tablespoons olive oil

1 yellow onion, finely diced

2 cloves garlic, minced

2 celery stalks, finely diced

1 carrot, peeled and grated

1½ teaspoons kosher salt

1 pound lean ground beef
(90 percent lean)

1 pound lean ground pork

1 (28-ounce) can whole
San Marzano tomatoes
and their liquid

½ cup dry red wine

¼ cup tomato paste

2 bay leaves

½ teaspoon freshly ground
black pepper

2 pounds fettuccine or
pasta shape of choice,
cooked and kept hot

Grated Parmesan cheese,
for serving

Classic Bolognese sauce usually simmers for 2 to 3 hours, but it is ready in less than an hour in the Instant Pot! You can make the sauce at dinnertime, or you can put it together in the morning and leave it unattended on the Keep Warm setting all day long. Then all you need to do is boil some pasta and dinner is served.

To make the Bolognese sauce, select the **Sauté** setting on the Instant Pot and heat the oil. Add the onion, garlic, celery, carrot, and salt and sauté for about 5 minutes, until the onion has softened and is translucent. Add the beef and pork and sauté, breaking them up with a wooden spoon or spatula as they cook, for about 10 minutes, until cooked through and no traces of pink remain.

Add the tomatoes and their liquid, crushing the tomatoes with your hands as you add them to the pot. Stir in the wine, tomato paste, bay leaves, and pepper.

Secure the lid and set the Pressure Release to **Sealing**. Press the **Cancel** button to reset the cooking program, then select the **Meat/Stew** setting and set the cooking time for 35 minutes at high pressure.

When the timer goes off, you have two choices: you can perform a quick release by moving the Pressure Release to **Venting** and serve the sauce right away, or you can let the pressure release naturally and leave the sauce in the Instant Pot on the **Keep Warm** setting for up to 10 hours.

Open the pot and taste and adjust the seasoning with salt and pepper if needed. Spoon the sauce over the pasta, sprinkle with the Parmesan, and serve.

MEATBALLS MARINARA

SERVES 4 (MAKES
ABOUT 20 MEATBALLS)

1 pound lean ground beef
(90 percent lean)

1 large egg

½ cup dried bread crumbs

1 teaspoon Italian
seasoning

1 teaspoon kosher salt

3 cups marinara sauce,
homemade (page 153)
or store-bought

½ cup water

Here's a quick weeknight dinner, whether you are making the meatballs after you get home from work or you are moving already-made uncooked meatballs directly from the freezer to the Instant Pot (see Note). The recipe can be easily multiplied, too, so make a double or triple batch and store the extras for another day. While the meatballs are cooking, sauté a big batch of greens or spiralized zucchini on the stove top or put on a pot of water to boil for pasta, and serve the meatballs with the greens or pasta.

In a bowl, combine the beef, egg, bread crumbs, Italian seasoning, and salt and mix with your hands until all of the ingredients are evenly distributed. Shape the mixture into about 20 meatballs, each about the size of a golf ball (about 1½ tablespoons).

Pour the marinara sauce and water into the Instant Pot and stir to mix well. Add the meatballs in a single layer, spooning the sauce over the meatballs so they are fully covered by the sauce.

Secure the lid and set the Pressure Release to **Sealing**. Select the **Manual** setting and set the cooking time for 20 minutes at high pressure.

Let the pressure release naturally for at least 10 minutes, then move the Pressure Release to **Venting** to release any remaining steam.

Open the pot and serve the meatballs and sauce on their own or with sautéed greens, sautéed spiralized zucchini, or cooked pasta of your choice.

NOTE To freeze the meatballs, line a sheet pan with plastic wrap, parchment paper, or a silicone baking mat. Make the meatball mixture and shape into balls as directed, arranging the balls on the prepared pan as they are ready. Slip the pan into the freezer for about 3 hours, until the balls are frozen solid. Transfer the balls to ziplock plastic freezer bags and seal closed, pressing out any excess air, then place the bag in the freezer. They will keep for up to 4 months. When it is time to cook them, transfer them directly from the freezer to the Instant Pot and cook as directed.

HOW TO FREEZE MEAT FOR THE INSTANT POT

The thinner the cut of meat, the better the result. Think chicken thighs or small- to average-size breasts, thin-cut pork chops, flank or skirt steak, or small fish fillets. Larger cuts, such as a pot roast, a whole chicken, or a pork shoulder roast won't work well straight out of the freezer.

Break down larger cuts of meat and freeze the smaller pieces in advance. Let's say you find a great deal on a big roast, but you won't be able to use it this week. When you get it home from the store, cut it into 1-inch or smaller pieces, then spread the pieces in a single layer on a sheet pan and pop the pan into the freezer for about 2 hours, or until the meat is frozen solid. Transfer the frozen pieces to a ziplock plastic freezer bag and store in the freezer for up to 6 months. The meat will be great for a stew or chili.

Freeze ground meat and sausage in a thin layer. Put 1 pound of ground meat or bulk sausage into a 1-gallon ziplock plastic freezer bag. Then, using your hands or a rolling pin, flatten the meat into a thin, even layer. Seal the bag and place in the freezer for up to 4 months. When you are ready to use the meat, it is easy to break up the thin sheet into smaller pieces. These small, thin pieces will thaw relatively quickly when browned on the **Sauté** setting.

Boil, don't braise (or steam). Frozen meats cook most evenly and efficiently when completely submerged in liquid. You'll have the most success with soups, stews, chilis, and chowders, that is, with recipes in which you cover the ingredients completely with cooking liquid (usually water or broth). The liquid conducts heat more efficiently than steam does, so if the meat is completely covered, it has a better chance of cooking all the way to the center.

Allow extra time for the pressure to build and a little more time to cook the meat. Frozen ingredients will lower the temperature in the Instant Pot. That means it will take a bit longer for the liquid to boil and build up pressure in the pot. In general, for thin cuts and small pieces of meat and for ground meat broken into small pieces, add 5 minutes to the recipe cooking time.

IRISH BEEF AND ROOT VEGETABLE STEW

Beer makes a great beef stew even better. A glug of Guinness (or any other stout) adds a little extra something to this hearty bowl of beef, mushrooms, onions, and root vegetables. If you prefer to leave out the beer, use beef broth in its place. You can also use this recipe for oxtails, lamb shanks, or really for any braising cut! Just add an extra 10 minutes of cooking time for larger, on-the-bone cuts.

SERVES 4

Sprinkle the beef all over with the salt and pepper. Select the **Sauté** setting on the Instant Pot and heat the oil. Add the onion, garlic, and mushrooms and sauté for about 5 minutes, until the onion has softened and is translucent.

Add the Guinness, Worcestershire sauce, mustard, tomato paste, rosemary, and bay leaf and mix well. Bring the mixture to a simmer, then stir in the beef.

Secure the lid and set the Pressure Release to **Sealing**. Press the **Cancel** button to reset the cooking program, then select the **Meat/Stew** setting and set the cooking time for 30 minutes at high pressure.

Let the pressure release naturally for at least 10 minutes, then move the Pressure Release to **Venting** to release any remaining steam. At this point, you can leave the stew on the **Keep Warm** setting for up to 10 hours.

Open the pot, remove the bay leaf, and stir in the carrots, parsnip, and rutabaga. Secure the lid once again and set the Pressure Release to **Sealing**. Press the **Cancel** button to reset the cooking program, then select the **Manual** setting and set the cooking time for 3 minutes at high pressure.

Perform a quick release by moving the Pressure Release to **Venting**.

In a small bowl, stir together the cornstarch and water, mixing well. Open the pot and quickly stir the cornstarch mixture into the stew. Re-cover and let stand for about 5 minutes to thicken. Ladle the stew into bowls and serve.

1½ pounds boneless beef stew meat, in 1-inch cubes (chuck, shoulder, or other good cut for braising)

1 teaspoon kosher salt

¾ teaspoon freshly ground black pepper

2 tablespoons avocado oil or other neutral oil with high smoke point

1 yellow onion, diced

3 cloves garlic, chopped

8 ounces button or cremini mushrooms, quartered

1 cup Guinness or other stout

2 tablespoons Worcestershire sauce

1 tablespoon Dijon mustard

1 tablespoon tomato paste

1 teaspoon dried rosemary, crumbled, or 1 tablespoon chopped fresh rosemary

1 bay leaf

3 large carrots, peeled and sliced crosswise, ½ inch thick

1 large parsnip, peeled, quartered lengthwise, and sliced crosswise, ½ inch thick

1 rutabaga, peeled and cut into ½-inch dice

1 tablespoon cornstarch

1 tablespoon water

UNSTUFFED PEPPERS

SERVES 4

2 tablespoons olive oil

1 medium yellow
onion, diced

2 cloves garlic, chopped

1 pound lean ground beef
(90 percent lean)

1 tablespoon Italian
seasoning

1 teaspoon kosher salt

½ teaspoon freshly ground
black pepper

½ teaspoon red pepper
flakes

1 cup low-sodium chicken
broth (page 154)

1 tablespoon tomato paste

1 cup long-grain white rice

1 (15-ounce) can petite diced
tomatoes and their liquid

3 red, orange, and/or yellow
bell peppers, seeded and
cut into 1-inch squares

½ cup shredded mozzarella
cheese (optional)

Much easier to make than stuffed peppers, this one-pot dinner layers everything that typically goes into that recipe into the pot together. It's a flavorful jumble of ground beef, Italian seasoning, vegetables, and rice, great as is or with a topping of melted mozzarella.

Select the **Sauté** setting on the Instant Pot and heat the oil. Add the onion and garlic and sauté for about 5 minutes, until the onion has softened and is translucent. Add the beef, Italian seasoning, salt, black pepper, and pepper flakes and sauté, breaking up the beef with a wooden spoon or spatula as it cooks, for about 8 minutes, until cooked through and no traces of pink remain.

While the beef is cooking, stir together the chicken broth and tomato paste in a liquid measuring cup or small bowl. You can use the back of a spoon to mash up the tomato paste against the side of the cup so it breaks up and mixes in more easily.

Once the beef has cooked through, sprinkle the rice over the top of it in an even layer. Pour the broth mixture over the rice, then spread out the diced tomatoes on top. Finally, sprinkle on the chopped bell peppers in an even layer.

Secure the lid and set the Pressure Release to **Sealing**. Press the **Cancel** button to reset the cooking program, then select the **Manual** setting and set the cooking time for 8 minutes at high pressure.

Let the pressure release naturally for 15 minutes, then move the Pressure Release to **Venting** to release any remaining steam.

Open the pot and spoon the unstuffed peppers into individual bowls, making sure to dig down to the bottom of the pot so each person gets an equal amount of peppers, rice, and meat. Top with the cheese, if using, and serve.

CLASSIC MEAT LOAF

This meat loaf cooks in a cake pan that fits snugly in the Instant Pot. You can make it up to 10 hours before you're ready to eat, leaving it on the Keep Warm setting. Just before serving, pop the meat loaf under the broiler to warm the sweet and tangy glaze.

Lightly grease a 7-inch cake pan with olive oil or nonstick cooking spray. In a bowl, combine the beef, bread crumbs, onion, egg, Worcestershire sauce, mustard, salt, and pepper and mix well with your hands until all of the ingredients are evenly distributed. Transfer the meat mixture to the prepared pan, shaping it into an even layer. Cover the pan tightly with aluminum foil.

Fold a 20-inch-long sheet of aluminum foil in half lengthwise twice to create a 3-inch-wide strip. Center it underneath the pan to act as a sling for lifting the pan in and out of the Instant Pot. Pour 1 cup water into the pot and add the trivet.

Holding the ends of the foil sling, lift the cake pan and lower it into the pot. Fold over the ends of the sling so they fit inside the pot. Secure the lid and set the Pressure Release to **Sealing**. Select the **Manual** setting and set the cooking time for 20 minutes at high pressure. Perform a quick release by moving the Pressure Release to **Venting**.

While the pressure is releasing, make the glaze. In a small bowl, stir together the ketchup, sugar, and mustard, mixing well.

Open the pot and, wearing heat-resistant mitts, grasp the ends of the foil sling and lift the meat loaf out of the Instant Pot. Remove the foil covering the pan, then brush the glaze on top of the meat loaf.

Broil the meat loaf in a toaster oven (or a conventional oven) for a few minutes, just until the glaze becomes bubbly and browned. Cut into slices to serve.

SERVES 4

1 pound lean ground beef (90 percent lean)

¾ cup dried bread crumbs

1 small yellow onion, finely chopped

1 large egg

1 tablespoon Worcestershire sauce

1 tablespoon Dijon mustard

½ teaspoon kosher salt

½ teaspoon freshly ground black pepper

1 cup water

GLAZE

¼ cup ketchup

2 tablespoons brown sugar

1 teaspoon Dijon mustard

KOREAN BRAISED BEEF SHORT RIBS (GALBIJJIM)

I like to make *galbijjim*, the popular Korean comfort-food dish, with boneless beef short ribs. It's less traditional than using bone-in ribs, but hey, so is cooking the ribs in a pressure cooker! This recipe requires no browning step, since the sauce has plenty of deep flavor from the garlic, ginger, and soy sauce.

———————————

Pat the ribs dry with paper towels. Cut crosswise into 3-inch pieces and add them to the Instant Pot.

In a blender or food processor, combine the onion, pear, garlic, ginger, brown sugar, mirin, and soy sauce and process until smooth. Pour the sauce over the short ribs and stir to coat evenly. Arrange the rib pieces in a single layer. Secure the lid and set the Pressure Release to **Sealing**. Select the **Meat/Stew** setting for 35 minutes at high pressure.

When the timer goes off, you can either perform a quick release by moving the Pressure Release to **Venting**, or you can let the pressure release naturally, then leave the ribs in the Instant Pot on the **Keep Warm** setting for up to 10 hours.

Open the pot and stir in the carrots and daikon. Secure the lid once again and set the Pressure Release to **Sealing**. Press the **Cancel** button to reset the cooking program, then select the **Manual** program and set the cooking time for 3 minutes at high pressure. Perform a quick release by moving the Pressure Release to **Venting**. Open the pot and, using a slotted spoon, transfer the meat and vegetables to a serving dish and keep warm. Use a ladle or large spoon to skim the fat from the sauce.

In a bowl, stir together the cornstarch and water. Press the **Cancel** button to reset the cooking program, then select the **Sauté** setting. When the sauce comes to a simmer, stir in the cornstarch mixture and let it boil for 1 minute, until the sauce has thickened, then press the **Cancel** button to turn off the Instant Pot.

Spoon the thickened sauce over the meat and vegetables. Sprinkle the sesame seeds and green onions on top and serve.

SERVES 6 TO 8

3 to 3½ pounds boneless beef short ribs

1 yellow onion, cut into 1-inch pieces

1 Asian or Bosc pear (about 6 ounces), peeled, quartered, and cored

8 cloves garlic

1-inch knob fresh ginger, peeled and chopped

1 tablespoon brown sugar

¼ cup mirin (sweet rice wine) or apple juice

¼ cup soy sauce

4 large carrots, peeled and cut into 1-inch pieces

1 small daikon (about 1 pound), peeled and cut into 1-inch pieces

1 tablespoon cornstarch or arrowroot powder

1 tablespoon water

1 tablespoon sesame seeds

2 green onions, white and green parts, thinly sliced on the diagonal

NOTE For an even more colorful and filling meal, serve over a bed of rice, shredded Napa cabbage, and peppers.

ROPA VIEJA

1 (2-pound) boneless chuck roast

1½ teaspoons kosher salt

1 teaspoon freshly ground black pepper

4 tablespoons avocado oil or other neutral oil with high smoke point

2 bay leaves

1 cup beef broth

4 cloves garlic, chopped

1 large yellow onion, halved through the stem end, then sliced into half-moons

1 pasilla chile, seeded and sliced lengthwise into strips

1 yellow bell pepper, seeded and sliced lengthwise into strips

1 red bell pepper, seeded and sliced lengthwise into strips

2 tablespoons tomato paste

1 teaspoon ground cumin

Ropa vieja—literally "old clothes"—is a long-cooked Cuban dish of shredded beef and peppers. Here, I have speeded up the process by pressure-braising the meat in the Instant Pot, shredding it into strips, and then cooking it with a mixture of peppers and onion. The dish gets its name from its resemblance to torn well-worn clothing, but I promise that it tastes better than it sounds! Serve it with steamed rice, crusty bread, or baked sweet potatoes or plantains.

Season the chuck roast on all sides with the salt and pepper. Select the **Sauté** setting on the Instant Pot and heat 2 tablespoons of the oil. Using tongs, lower the roast into the pot and sear for 5 minutes on the first side. Using the tongs, flip the roast and sear on the second side for 5 minutes. The roast should be nicely browned on both sides. Add the bay leaves and broth.

Secure the lid and set the Pressure Release to **Sealing**. Press the **Cancel** button to reset the cooking program, then select the **Manual** setting and set the cooking time for 45 minutes at high pressure.

Perform a quick release by moving the Pressure Release to **Venting**. Open the pot and discard the bay leaves. Using the tongs, transfer the roast to a carving board. Wearing heat-resistant mitts, lift out the inner pot and pour the cooking liquid into a liquid measuring cup. Use two forks to shred the meat into strips.

Return the now-empty inner pot to the Instant Pot housing. Select the **Sauté** setting and heat the remaining 2 tablespoons oil. Add the garlic, onion, chile, and bell peppers and sauté for 5 minutes, until the onion has softened and is translucent. Add the tomato paste and cumin and sauté for 1 minute longer. Return the meat to the pot, then pour in 1 cup of the reserved cooking liquid. Secure the lid and set the Pressure Release to **Sealing**. Press the **Cancel** button to reset the cooking program, then select the **Manual** setting and set the cooking time for 15 minutes at high pressure.

Perform a quick release by moving the Pressure Release to **Venting**, then open the pot and serve.

SLOPPY JOES

This classic comfort-food dinner is one of my husband's favorites. He likes it so much that he probably wouldn't mind eating it most nights of the week! The Instant Pot will keep the Sloppy Joe mixture warm for hours, so it is a great dish for nights when everyone needs to eat dinner at a different time. Each diner can just waltz into the kitchen and ladle some Sloppy Joe mixture straight from the pot onto a toasted hamburger bun.

———————————

Select the **Sauté** setting on the Instant Pot and heat the oil. Add the beef and sauté, breaking it up with a wooden spoon or spatula as it cooks, for about 8 minutes, until cooked through and no traces of pink remain.

Stir in the yellow onion, carrots, celery, bell pepper, garlic, and salt and sauté for 10 more minutes, until the vegetables have softened and are giving up their liquid. Add the tomato sauce, tomato paste, vinegar, Worcestershire sauce, sugar, ground pepper, and nutmeg and stir well.

Secure the lid and set the Pressure Release to **Sealing**. Press the **Cancel** button to reset the cooking program, then select the **Bean/Chili** setting and set the cooking time for 20 minutes at high pressure.

You can perform a quick release by moving the Pressure Release to **Venting**, or you can let the pressure release naturally and leave the pot on the **Keep Warm** setting for up to 10 hours.

Open the pot and stir the Sloppy Joe mixture one last time. Place the bun bottoms, cut side up, on individual plates and ladle the Sloppy Joe mixture onto the buns. Top with the red onion and pickles, close with the bun tops, and serve hot.

NOTE Like many pressure cooker recipes, the Sloppy Joe mixture may look a little soupy when you first open the pot, but it sets up and thickens within a minute or two after stirring it. Feel free to mix in a little extra tomato paste or a dollop or two of ketchup if you like yours even thicker.

SERVES 4

2 tablespoons avocado oil or other neutral oil with high smoke point

1 pound lean ground beef (90 percent lean)

1 large yellow onion, diced

2 carrots, peeled and diced

4 celery stalks, diced

1 green bell pepper, seeded and diced

2 cloves garlic, chopped

½ teaspoon kosher salt

1 cup tomato sauce

2 tablespoons tomato paste

1 tablespoon cider vinegar

1½ teaspoons Worcestershire sauce

2 tablespoons brown sugar

½ teaspoon freshly ground black pepper

¼ teaspoon ground nutmeg

4 hamburger buns, split and toasted

Thinly sliced red onion, for serving

Sandwich pickle slices, for serving

SALISBURY STEAK

SERVES 4

PATTIES

1 pound lean ground beef
(90 percent lean)

⅓ cup dried bread crumbs

1 large egg

½ teaspoon kosher salt

¼ teaspoon freshly ground
black pepper

2 tablespoons avocado oil
or other neutral oil with
high smoke point

1 small yellow onion, sliced

1 clove garlic, chopped

¾ cup mushroom
duxelles (page 149), or
8 ounces cremini or button
mushrooms, sliced, and
½ teaspoon salt

2 tablespoons tomato paste

1½ teaspoons prepared
yellow mustard

1 cup low-sodium beef
broth, homemade
(page 155) or store-bought

2 teaspoons cornstarch

2 teaspoons water

2 tablespoons chopped
fresh flat-leaf parsley
(optional)

Cooked egg noodles
or Cauliflower Mashed
Potatoes (page 118),
for serving

I love a good retro recipe redux. Here, old-fashioned Salisbury steak gets a modern update from homemade bone broth and duxelles. Make these components ahead of time so you are ready to make this upgraded classic on a weeknight! If you've lacked the time to make them, you can use store-bought broth and fresh mushrooms.

To make the patties, in a bowl, combine the beef, bread crumbs, egg, salt, and pepper and mix with your hands until all of the ingredients are evenly distributed. Divide the mixture into four equal portions, then shape the portions into oval patties each ½ inch thick.

Select the **Sauté** setting on the Instant Pot, adjust the heat to **More**, and heat the oil. Add the patties and sear on the first side for 3 minutes, until browned. Using a thin, flexible spatula, flip the patties and brown on the second side for 2 to 3 minutes, until browned. Transfer the patties to a plate.

Add the onion and garlic to the pot and sauté for about 4 minutes, until the onion has softened. Add the duxelles and stir to combine. If using fresh mushrooms instead of duxelles, add the fresh mushrooms and ½ teaspoon salt to the pot with the onion and garlic and increase the sauté time to about 8 minutes, until the mushrooms have shrunk and given up their liquid.

Add the tomato paste, mustard, and broth and stir with a wooden spoon, using it to nudge any browned bits from the pot bottom. Return the patties to the pot in a single layer, spooning a bit of the sauce over each one.

Secure the lid and set the Pressure Release to **Sealing**. Press the **Cancel** button to reset the cooking program, then select the **Manual** setting and set the cooking time for 10 minutes at high pressure.

Let the pressure release naturally for 10 minutes, then move the Pressure Release to **Venting** to release any remaining steam. Open the pot and transfer the patties to a serving plate.

In a small bowl, stir together the cornstarch and water. Press the **Cancel** button to reset the cooking program once again, then select the **Sauté** setting. When the sauce comes to a simmer, stir in the cornstarch mixture and let it boil for about 1 minute, until the sauce has thickened, then press the **Cancel** button to turn off the Instant Pot.

Spoon the sauce over the patties and sprinkle with the parsley. Serve hot with the noodles on the side.

NOTE If you are not serving the Salisbury Steak right away, let the pressure release naturally and then leave everything in the pot on the Keep Warm setting for up to 10 hours. When you are ready to serve, open the pot, transfer the patties to a plate, and proceed as directed to thicken the sauce and serve the dish.

BBQ BABY BACK RIBS

SERVES 4

1 or 2 racks baby back ribs, 2½ to 3½ pounds total

4 cups apple juice

½ cup cider vinegar

½ cup favorite barbecue sauce

Making a batch of barbecued ribs in the Instant Pot is much faster than doing it on the grill, and you can make them any time of the year. The ribs cook to tenderness in the pot, then get brushed with barbecue sauce and take a quick trip to the oven until nicely browned and caramelized.

With a rack bone side up, and starting at one end, slip a knife tip under the translucent membrane, loosening it from the bone. Once you have lifted enough to get a good grip, grasp the membrane with a paper towel and peel it off the rack (or ask your butcher to do this). Repeat with the remaining rack(s). Cut the rack(s) in half crosswise.

Stack the ribs in the Instant Pot. Pour in the apple juice and vinegar. Secure the lid and move the Pressure Release to **Sealing**. Select the **Meat/Stew** setting and set the cooking time for 20 minutes at high pressure. (For meat-falling-off-the-bone ribs, set the cooking time for 25 minutes.)

Let the pressure release naturally for 15 minutes. While the pressure is releasing, preheat the oven to 400°F and line a sheet pan with aluminum foil or a silicone baking mat.

When 15 minutes have passed, move the Pressure Release to **Venting** to release any remaining steam. Open the pot and, using a pair of tongs, transfer the ribs to the prepared sheet pan. Discard the cooking liquid.

Brush the ribs on both sides with the barbecue sauce, then bake for about 10 minutes, until the sauce is a caramelized and browned. Remove from the oven, cut the ribs apart, and serve.

NOTE You can steam the ribs with water instead of braising them in the apple juice and vinegar. They will be slightly less flavorful but still good. To steam the ribs, pour 1 cup water into the Instant Pot, place the trivet in the pot, arrange the ribs on top of the trivet, and secure the lid. Select the Steam setting and set the cooking time for 20 or 25 minutes at high pressure, depending on how well-done you like your ribs. Release the pressure and bake the ribs as directed.

BRAISED BRISKET WITH ONION GRAVY

1 beef brisket, 2½ to
3½ pounds

1½ teaspoons kosher salt

½ teaspoon freshly ground
black pepper

1 tablespoon avocado oil or
other neutral oil with high
smoke point

3 yellow onions, sliced

3 large cloves garlic

½ cup water

½ cup dry red wine

3 tablespoons tomato paste

1 teaspoon dried rosemary

1 teaspoon dried thyme

1 teaspoon sweet paprika

I grew up eating long-braised brisket, the kind that takes at least three hours in the oven, low and slow. This version cooks in about half the time and is just as good. The braising liquid becomes a rich onion gravy and makes enough for spooning over mashed potatoes, an ideal side dish.

―――――――――――

Pat the brisket dry with paper towels. If the fat layer on the top of the brisket is more than ¼ inch thick, trim off the excess. Season the brisket on both sides with ½ teaspoon of the salt and all of the ground pepper.

Select the **Sauté** setting on the Instant Pot, adjust the heat level to **More**, and heat the oil. With tongs, lower the brisket, fat side down, into the pot. Let it sear for 6 minutes on the first side, then turn the brisket over and sear for 6 more minutes. Transfer the brisket to a serving plate.

Press the **Cancel** button to reset the cooking program, then select the **Sauté** setting again and this time leave it on the default (**Normal**) heat setting. Add the onions, garlic, and the remaining 1 teaspoon salt and sauté, stirring to dislodge any browned bits from the pot bottom, for about 10 minutes, until the onions are softened. Stir in the water, wine, tomato paste, rosemary, thyme, and paprika. Using the tongs, lower the brisket back into the pot.

Secure the lid and set the Pressure Release to **Sealing**. Press the **Cancel** button to reset the cooking program, then select the **Meat/Stew** setting and set the cooking time for 50 minutes at high pressure.

Perform a quick release by moving the Pressure Release to **Venting**, or let the pressure release naturally (this will take about 25 minutes). You can then open the pot or you can leave the brisket in the pot on the **Keep Warm** setting for up to 10 hours.

Transfer the brisket to a carving board or plate. Set a fine-mesh strainer over a bowl. Wearing heat-resistant mitts, lift the inner pot out of the Instant Pot and strain the cooking liquid into the bowl. Return the garlic and onions to the inner pot.

Pour the cooking liquid into a fat separator, then pour the cooking liquid from the fat separator back into the inner pot, discarding the layer of fat left behind. Alternatively, scoop off the fat from the surface with a ladle or large spoon, or chill the cooking liquid until the fat solidifies, then lift off and discard the fat.

With an immersion blender, blend together the cooking liquid, onions, and garlic until smooth. To prevent splattering and to blend the sauce evenly, you may need to tilt the pot toward you so the blender head is completely submerged in the sauce. Place the inner pot back in the Instant Pot housing to keep the gravy warm.

Carve the brisket crosswise into ¼-inch-thick slices. Serve the brisket right away with the gravy poured over the top, or return the slices to the Instant Pot and leave the pot on the **Keep Warm** setting until you're ready to serve.

NOTE There are two kinds of brisket cuts, the point (aka the deckle) and the flat. Use the point cut if you like fattier, richer brisket. Choose the flat cut if you prefer your brisket very lean.

ONE-POT ROAST DINNER

SERVES 4 TO 6

1 boneless chuck roast,
2½ to 3½ pounds

1 teaspoon kosher salt

1 teaspoon freshly ground
black pepper

1 tablespoon avocado oil or
other neutral oil with high
smoke point

1 large yellow onion, sliced

8 ounces cremini or button
mushrooms, quartered

3 cloves garlic, smashed

1 cup beef broth,
homemade (page 155)
or store-bought

½ cup dry red wine

2 tablespoons tomato paste

1 tablespoon Dijon mustard

½ teaspoon dried thyme

½ teaspoon dried oregano

1 pound carrots, peeled and
sliced ½ inch thick

1½ pounds small waxy
potatoes, halved or
quartered (1-inch pieces)

A chuck roast takes hours to cook in the oven, but it gets fall-apart tender in just over an hour in the Instant Pot. You'll sear the roast, then let it braise over onions, mushrooms, garlic, and a flavorful cooking liquid. Cooking the pot roast on the Instant Pot trivet makes it easy to remove the roast from the pot. It will be so tender that, if not on the trivet, it might otherwise fall apart.

———————————

Season the roast on all sides with the salt and pepper. Put the Instant Pot trivet on a plate.

Select the **Sauté** setting on the Instant Pot and heat the oil. Using tongs, lower the roast into the pot and sear for about 5 minutes, until browned on the first side. Using the tongs, flip the roast and sear on the second side for about 5 minutes, until browned. Again using the tongs, transfer the roast to the trivet.

Add the onion, mushrooms, and garlic to the now-empty pot and sauté for 5 minutes, until the onions have softened a bit and are translucent. Add the broth, wine, tomato paste, mustard, thyme, and oregano, stir well, and let come to a simmer.

When the liquid begins to simmer, use the trivet to lower the roast into the pot. It is fine that it is not submerged fully in the liquid. Secure the lid and set the Pressure Release to **Sealing**. Press the **Cancel** button to reset the cooking program, then select the **Meat/Stew** setting and set the cooking time for 55 minutes at high pressure.

When the cooking program finishes, you can let the pressure release naturally for 15 minutes, then move the Pressure Release to **Venting** to release any remaining steam, or you can let the pressure release naturally (this will take about 30 minutes). You can then open the pot or you can leave the roast in the pot on the **Keep Warm** setting for up to 10 hours.

Wearing heat-resistant mitts, lift the trivet, with the pot roast on top, out of the pot. Transfer the roast to a carving board or plate and tent with aluminum foil to keep it warm.

Place a wire-mesh strainer over a large (1- to 2-quart) liquid measuring cup or a bowl with a pouring spout. Still wearing the mitts, lift the inner pot out of the Instant Pot and strain the cooking liquid into the bowl. Return the cooked onions, mushrooms, and garlic to the inner pot.

Pour the cooking liquid into a fat separator, then pour the liquid from the separator back into the inner pot, discarding the layer of fat left behind. Alternatively, scoop off the fat from the surface with a ladle or large spoon, or chill the cooking liquid until the fat solidifies, then lift off and discard the fat.

Return the inner pot to the Instant Pot and stir in the carrots and potatoes. Secure the lid and set the Pressure Release to **Sealing**. Press the **Cancel** button to reset the cooking program, then select the **Manual** setting and set the cooking time for 5 minutes at high pressure.

Perform a quick release by moving the Pressure Release to **Venting**, then open the pot. Transfer the vegetables to a serving dish.

Carve the pot roast into ½-inch-thick slices and serve with the vegetables. Top the meat and vegetables with a generous ladleful of the cooking liquid.

NOTE If you prefer, you can serve your pot roast with mashed potatoes or noodles instead of cooking potatoes in the sauce. You can cook only the carrots or omit both the potatoes and carrots. Proceed as directed, serving the roast with the braised vegetables and the defatted cooking liquid.

PULLED PORK ADOBO

Pork shoulder recipes are abundant in the world of pressure cooking for a reason: they make fantastic use of the Instant Pot's quick-cooking powers, which turn this tough braising cut tender and easy to shred in less than an hour. Flavorful, saucy pork adobo makes a great taco, burrito, or tamale filling or a good main course with sides of rice and beans. The sauce recipe yields twice as much as you need for pork, but the extra batch freezes well. Any leftover pork will keep too, for up to a couple of days in the refrigerator or up to 3 months in the freezer.

———————————

To make the sauce, bring a kettle of water to a boil on the stove top. Place the ancho and guajillo chiles in a heatproof bowl, add boiling water to cover, and let soak for 20 minutes, until softened. Remove the chiles from the water, remove their stems, split them in half lengthwise, and scrape out their seeds and ribs. Discard the soaking water.

In a blender, combine the chiles, garlic, onion, salt, cumin, oregano, black pepper, cinnamon, cayenne, and orange juice and process until a smooth puree forms. You should have about 2 cups. Measure 1 cup for this recipe and set aside. Transfer the remainder to an airtight container and freeze for up to 3 months.

To cook the pork, cut the roast into 4-inch cubes—it is fine if they are a bit irregular—and season them with ½ teaspoon of the salt and all of the pepper.

Select the **Sauté** setting on the Instant Pot, adjust the heat level to **More**, and heat the oil. Using tongs, place the pork cubes in the pot. Sear the pork for about 6 minutes, until well browned on the first side. Flip the pieces over and sear for about 6 minutes longer, until well browned on the second side. Using the tongs, transfer the pork to a plate.

CONTINUED

SERVES **6** TO **8**

ADOBO SAUCE

4 ancho chiles

4 guajillo chiles

4 cloves garlic

1 yellow onion, cut into 1-inch pieces

1½ teaspoons kosher salt

½ teaspoon ground cumin

½ teaspoon oregano

½ teaspoon black pepper

½ teaspoon ground cinnamon

¼ teaspoon cayenne pepper

1 cup fresh orange juice

PORK

1 boneless pork shoulder roast, about 3 pounds

1 teaspoon kosher salt

½ teaspoon freshly ground black pepper

2 tablespoons avocado oil or other neutral oil with high smoke point

2 yellow onions, sliced

½ cup low-sodium chicken broth (page 154) or water

Add the onions and the remaining ½ teaspoon salt and sauté for about 5 minutes, until the onions have softened. Stir in the broth and the 1 cup adobo sauce, then return the seared pork to the pot and stir to coat it with the sauce. Arrange the pork pieces in a single layer.

Secure the lid and set the Pressure Release to **Sealing**. Press the **Cancel** button to reset the cooking program, then select the **Meat/Stew** setting and set the cooking time for 50 minutes at high pressure.

Perform a quick release by moving the Pressure Release to **Venting**. Open the pot and, using the tongs or a slotted spoon, transfer the pork to a carving board or large dish.

Press the **Cancel** button to reset the cooking program, then select the **Sauté** setting. Let the sauce simmer, uncovered, for 15 minutes. Meanwhile, use a pair of forks to shred the pork.

When the sauce is ready, return the shredded pork to the pot and stir to combine. At this point, you can select the **Keep Warm** setting to keep the sauce and meat warm for up to 10 hours before serving. Serve the pork right away, refrigerate it for up to 48 hours, or freeze it in ziplock bags for up to 4 months.

NOTES If you are pressed for time, substitute 1 cup of your favorite store-bought simmering sauce for the adobo sauce.

To make a smooth, thicker sauce, before adding the meat, use an immersion blender to blend the sauce. To prevent splattering and to blend the sauce evenly, wearing heat-resistant mitts, lift the inner pot out of the housing, then tilt the pot to make sure the immersion blender head is fully submerged in the sauce.

To make pork adobo tacos, warm corn tortillas and top them with the pork, sliced or pickled red onions, and fresh cilantro.

JAMAICAN JERK-SPICED OXTAILS

The thick, rich onion gravy in this recipe is sweet and spicy thanks to a
Caribbean-inspired blend of spices. Use either a store-bought jerk seasoning
blend or mix up your own (see Note). Substitute any long-cooking cut of beef
for the oxtails. Serve with Jamaican-Style Rice and Beans (page 41).

Season the oxtails on both sides with the salt and pepper. Select the **Sauté** setting
on the Instant Pot and heat the oil. Using tongs, place the oxtails in the pot in a
single layer and sear, turning once, for 4 minutes on each side, until browned.
Transfer to a plate. Add the onion, shallots, and garlic and sauté the onion and
shallots for about 5 minutes, until softened and translucent. Add the spice
blend, tomato paste, broth, vinegar, and Worcestershire sauce and stir well.
Return the oxtails to the pot, turning them around in the cooking liquid a bit,
and then nestle them in a single layer on top of the onions and cooking liquid.

Secure the lid and set the Pressure Release to **Sealing**. Press the **Cancel** button
to reset the cooking program, then select the **Meat/Stew** program and set the
cooking time for 55 minutes at high pressure.

Perform a quick release by moving the Pressure Release to **Venting**, or let the
pressure release naturally (this will take about 25 minutes). Open the pot and,
using tongs, transfer the oxtails to a serving dish. Wearing heat-resistant mitts,
lift the inner pot out of the Instant Pot and strain the cooking liquid into a fat
separator, reserving the onions, shallots, and garlic. If you don't have a fat separator, strain the cooking liquid through a fine-mesh strainer placed over a bowl
and scoop off the fat from the surface with a ladle or large spoon. (If making the
dish a day ahead, chill the strained liquid in the refrigerator until the fat solidifies
on top, then lift off the fat and discard it.) Pour the defatted cooking liquid back
into the inner pot and add the reserved onions, shallots, and garlic.

Using an immersion blender, blend the vegetables into the cooking liquid, tilting
the pot so the head of the blender is submerged in the liquid. Pour the blended
mixture over the oxtails and serve, or return the oxtails to the pot with the sauce
and leave on the **Keep Warm** setting for up to 10 hours, until ready to serve.

SERVES 4

2½ to 3 pounds oxtails,
trimmed of excess fat
if needed

1 teaspoon kosher salt

½ teaspoon freshly ground
black pepper

1 tablespoon coconut oil

1 yellow onion, sliced

4 large shallots (about
8 ounces), sliced

3 cloves garlic, smashed

2 tablespoons unsalted
Caribbean spice blend
(see Note)

2 tablespoons tomato paste

½ cup beef broth

1 tablespoon cider vinegar

1 tablespoon Worcestershire
sauce

NOTE To make a quick
Caribbean spice blend, in
a small bowl, stir together
2 teaspoons dried thyme,
1 teaspoon sweet paprika,
1 teaspoon ground allspice,
 ½ teaspoon ground black
pepper, ½ teaspoon red
pepper flakes, ¼ teaspoon
cayenne pepper,
¼ teaspoon ground
ginger, ¼ teaspoon ground
nutmeg, and ¼ teaspoon
ground cinnamon.

CORNED BEEF WITH CABBAGE, CARROTS, AND POTATOES

I like to buy and freeze a few packages of corned beef when it's on sale around St. Patrick's Day since it makes for such an easy meal. You can cook the corned beef in the Instant Pot any time during the day, then steam the vegetables in the same pot right before dinner.

SERVES 8

1 corned beef, 4 pounds (or smaller), with spice packet

6 cups water

1 pound small red potatoes (2 to 3 inches in diameter), quartered

1 pound carrots, peeled and cut into 1-inch pieces

1 small green cabbage (about 1½ pounds), cored and cut into wedges

---

Place the corned beef in the Instant Pot and add the contents of the spice packet and the water.

Secure the lid and set the Pressure Release to **Sealing**. Select the **Meat/Stew** setting and set the cooking time for 55 minutes at high pressure.

Let the pressure release naturally (this will take about 30 minutes). At this point, you can either continue with the recipe or you can leave the corned beef in the pot on the **Keep Warm** setting for up to 10 hours.

Open the pot and transfer the corned beef to a carving board. Tent the corned beef with aluminum foil to keep it warm. Wearing heat-resistant mitts, lift the inner pot out of the Instant Pot housing. Discard all but 2 cups of the cooking liquid, then return the inner pot with the liquid to the Instant Pot.

Place a steamer basket in the Instant Pot. Layer the vegetables in the basket: potatoes on the bottom, then the carrots, and finally the cabbage wedges on top. Secure the lid and set the Pressure Release to **Sealing**. Press the **Cancel** button to reset the cooking program, then select the **Steam** setting and set the cooking time for 5 minutes at high pressure.

Perform a quick release by moving the Pressure Release to **Venting**. Open the pot and transfer the vegetables to a serving dish.

Carve the corned beef into ¾-inch-thick slices and serve with the steamed vegetables.

PORK LOIN WITH BALSAMIC AND CARAMELIZED ONIONS

1 boneless pork loin roast, about 2 pounds

½ teaspoon kosher salt

½ teaspoon freshly ground black pepper

1 tablespoon avocado oil or other neutral oil with high smoke point

1 small yellow onion, sliced

1 clove garlic

½ cup balsamic vinegar

¼ cup water, plus 2 teaspoons

1 tablespoon Dijon mustard

1 tablespoon brown sugar

1 bay leaf

2 teaspoons cornstarch or arrowroot powder

The pork roast and onions are seared on high heat for lots of rich, caramelized flavor, and the balsamic vinegar gives the sauce an irresistible sweet-and-sour tanginess. Make sure you're using a pork *loin*, and not a pork *tenderloin*, for this recipe. The tenderloin cut is more delicate and lean, so it's better suited to stir-frying or high-heat roasting.

———————————

Season the pork on all sides with the salt and pepper.

Select the **Sauté** setting on the Instant pot, adjust the heat level to **More**, and heat the oil. Using tongs, lower the pork roast, fat side down, into the pot, then sear for about 6 minutes, until browned on the first side. Using the tongs, flip the roast and sear for about 6 minutes, until browned on the second side. Again using the tongs, transfer the roast to a plate.

Add the onion and garlic to the pot and sauté for 5 minutes, stirring to dislodge any browned bits from the pot bottom. Stir in the vinegar, ¼ cup of the water, the mustard, sugar, and bay leaf, mixing well. Using the tongs, return the roast to the pot and turn it to coat it in the cooking liquid.

Secure the lid and set the Pressure Release to **Sealing**. Press the **Cancel** button to reset the cooking program, then select the **Meat/Stew** setting and set the cooking time for 50 minutes at high pressure.

Perform a quick release by moving the Pressure Release to **Venting**, or let the pressure release naturally (this will take about 20 minutes). At this point, you can either continue with the recipe or you can leave the roast in the pot for up to 10 hours on the **Keep Warm** setting.

Set a fine-mesh strainer over a bowl. Open the pot and, wearing heat-resistant mitts, lift the inner pot out of the Instant Pot and strain the cooking liquid into the bowl. Return the garlic and onion to the inner pot. Pour the cooking liquid into a fat separator, then pour the cooking liquid from the fat separator back into the Instant Pot, discarding the layer of fat left behind. Alternatively, scoop off the fat from the surface with a ladle or large spoon, or chill the cooking liquid until the fat solidifies, then lift off and discard the fat.

Place the inner pot back in the Instant Pot housing. Press the **Cancel** button to reset the cooking program, then select the **Sauté** setting. Meanwhile, in a small bowl, stir together the cornstarch and the remaining 2 teaspoons water. When the sauce begins to simmer, pour in the cornstarch mixture and stir for a minute or so, until slightly thickened. Press the **Keep Warm/Cancel** button to end the **Sauté** program and switch the Instant Pot to its **Keep Warm** setting.

Carve the pork loin into ½-inch-thick slices. Serve the pork right away with the sauce poured over the top, or return it to the Instant Pot and leave it on the **Keep Warm** setting until you're ready to serve.

CHAPTER 6

Vegetables
and
Side Dishes

STEAMED ARTICHOKES WITH QUICK MAYONNAISE

SERVES 4

4 medium globe artichokes (see Notes if using a different size)

1 cup water

Quick Mayonnaise (page 153)

NOTES You can steam artichokes of any size in the Instant Pot. The 6-quart models will accommodate 4 medium-to-large artichokes (3 to 4 inches in diameter at their widest point) or 2 jumbo artichokes (4½ to 5 inches in diameter). Set the cooking time for 10 minutes for medium artichokes, 12 minutes for large artichokes, and 15 minutes for jumbo artichokes.

Although the mayonnaise is easy to make, you can use your favorite store-bought mayonnaise in its place.

Artichokes should be tender and cooked through, but not waterlogged and mushy in the middle. It can be tricky to give an exact recommendation on their cooking time, as they vary dramatically in both size and freshness. In general, I have found that most suggested times for steaming artichokes in a pressure cooker are way too long, so I like to start with a shorter cooking time than usual. It's easy to test an artichoke for doneness, and then put it back into the pot for a minute if it's not yet done to your liking.

Prepare the artichokes one at a time: Holding an artichoke firmly on its side, use a serrated bread knife or very sharp chef's knife to cut off the top one-third of the leaves. Next, cut off the stem even with the bottom of the artichoke. With kitchen shears, trim off any thorny tips that remain on the leaves.

Pour the water into the Instant Pot and place a steamer basket in the pot. Place the artichokes in the basket. Secure the lid and set the Pressure Release to **Sealing**. Select the **Steam** setting and set the cooking time for 10 minutes at high pressure.

Let the pressure release naturally for 5 minutes, then move the Pressure Release to **Venting** to release any remaining steam.

Open the pot and test an artichoke for doneness by trying to pull out an inner leaf. If it releases easily, the artichokes are ready. If it is difficult to free it, the artichokes need to be cooked longer. In that case, secure the lid again, press the **Cancel** button to reset the cooking program, then select the **Steam** setting and cook for 1 minute. Let the pressure release naturally for 5 minutes, move the Pressure Release to **Venting** to release any remaining steam, open the pot, and test again for doneness. If it fails the doneness test again, cook for 1 minute longer, using the same process.

Using tongs, transfer the artichokes to individual serving plates, allowing any excess liquid to drain back into the pot. Serve them with the mayonnaise alongside for dipping.

STEAMED SPAGHETTI SQUASH

SERVES 4

1½ cups water

1 small-to-medium
spaghetti squash,
2½ to 3 pounds

Spaghetti squash is often touted as a delicious, low-carb alternative to pasta. I like to think of it more as a vegetable side dish with strands that are lighter and more delicate than noodles. You can serve it similarly to pasta, topped with spaghetti sauce; toss it with butter, salt, and pepper for a simple vegetable side dish; or use it in place of noodles in an Asian-style stir-fry.

Pour the water into the Instant Pot and place the trivet in the pot.

Cut the squash in half crosswise (not lengthwise; you want two short halves). Scoop out the seeds and discard them. Place the squash halves, cut side up, in the pot. If the squash is too big to fit in the pot this way, lop off the tough stem end and cut the squash into quarters. The quarters can then be nested in the pot in a single layer. If they don't fit in a single layer, steam the squash in two batches.

Secure the lid and set the Pressure Release to **Sealing**. Select the **Steam** setting and set the cooking time for 7 minutes at high pressure.

Perform a quick release by moving the Pressure Release to **Venting**.

Open the pot and test the squash for doneness with a fork. It should pierce the flesh with little effort, and you should be able to separate the flesh easily into spaghetti-like strands by dragging the fork tines over the flesh to separate the strands. (If the squash has not cooked through, secure the lid, set the Pressure Release to **Sealing**, select the **Steam** setting again, and cook for an additional 1 or 2 minutes, then perform a quick release.)

Using tongs or wearing heat-resistant gloves, carefully lift the cooked squash pieces out of the pot. When the squash is cool enough to handle, use a fork to scoop out the flesh, forming strands, and use as you like (see serving ideas on the next page).

SERVING IDEAS FOR SPAGHETTI SQUASH

With Marinara Sauce: Serve the squash with marinara sauce (page 153) and a sprinkle of Parmesan cheese on top.

Gratin: In a large bowl, stir together the cooked, cooled squash strands; 2 eggs, lightly beaten; ⅔ cup of your favorite grated melting cheese; ½ cup whole milk; ¼ cup chopped fresh herbs; ½ teaspoon kosher salt; and ¼ teaspoon freshly ground black pepper, mixing well. Transfer the mixture to a greased 2-quart baking dish. Top with buttered bread crumbs, cover with aluminum foil, and bake in a preheated 375°F oven for 30 minutes. Uncover and continue to bake for 10 minutes longer, until bubbly and browned on top. Let cool for a few minutes before serving.

Chow Mein Style: In a large skillet, heat 1 tablespoon avocado oil or other neutral oil with a high smoke point over medium-high heat. Add 3 cloves garlic, minced, and sauté for about 2 minutes, until lightly golden. Toss in the cooked spaghetti squash; 4 green onions, sliced (white and green parts); 3 celery stalks, thinly sliced; 1 cup shredded carrots; and 3 tablespoons soy sauce and sauté for about 3 minutes, until the vegetables are just cooked through. Top with chopped fresh cilantro and serve hot.

WARM FINGERLING POTATO SALAD

SERVES 6

2 cups water

1½ pounds fingerling potatoes

3 tablespoons olive oil

1 red onion, diced

3 tablespoons cider vinegar

2 tablespoons capers, rinsed and drained

2 teaspoons Dijon mustard

½ teaspoon freshly ground black pepper

¼ teaspoon kosher salt

½ cup chopped fresh flat-leaf parsley

¼ chopped fresh chives

I had been making this potato salad for years before I adapted it for the Instant Pot. It's easier and faster than my original method, and you've only got one pot to wash when you're done. Fingerling potatoes hold their shape well when steamed, making them perfect for salad. Coated with a warm cider vinegar dressing, they're irresistible. Capers, Dijon mustard, and kosher salt ensure a robustly seasoned salad, while the parsley and chives nicely cut the richness of the dressing.

———————————

Pour the water into the Instant Pot. Place a steamer basket in the pot and add the potatoes to the basket.

Secure the lid and set the Pressure Release to **Sealing**. Select the **Steam** setting and set the cooking time for 5 minutes at high pressure.

Perform a quick pressure release by moving the Pressure Release to **Venting**. Open the pot and, wearing heat-resistant mitts, lift out the steamer basket of potatoes, and let them cool for about 10 minutes, just until you are able to handle them comfortably. Then, still wearing the mitts, lift out the inner pot, pour off all of the water, and return the inner pot to the Instant Pot housing.

While the potatoes are cooling, press the **Cancel** button to reset the cooking program, then select the **Sauté** setting and heat the oil. Add the onion and sauté for about 10 minutes, until softened and just beginning to brown.

Press the **Cancel** button to turn off the Instant Pot. Add the vinegar, capers, mustard, pepper, and salt and stir well.

Slice the potatoes into ¼-inch-thick rounds, then return them to the pot. Add the parsley and chives and stir gently until the potatoes are evenly coated with the dressing. Transfer the salad to a serving bowl and serve warm or at room temperature.

WINTER VEGETABLE MASH (STAMPPOT)

In 2012, my friend Katy was living in the Netherlands, and she didn't have a lot of nice things to say about Dutch food. She asked me to come up with an improved version of *stamppot*, a traditional winter side dish of potatoes mashed with root vegetables and/or greens, and I was happy to oblige. This simple recipe is even faster in the Instant Pot, and I think of Katy every time I make it. Serve it with sausages and sauerkraut for a comforting weeknight meal, or as an alternative to mashed potatoes on your holiday table.

SERVES 6 TO 8

4 tablespoons unsalted butter or ghee

1 large leek, dark green ends discarded, halved lengthwise, thinly sliced crosswise, and rinsed well (about 6 ounces trimmed)

1 teaspoon kosher salt

½ small green cabbage (1 pound), cored and sliced into ¼-inch-wide ribbons

1½ pounds waxy potatoes, peeled and cut into 1-inch pieces

3 large carrots (about 8 ounces total), peeled and sliced ½ inch thick

2 parsnips (about 12 ounces total), peeled and diced

1 rutabaga (8 to 12 ounces), peeled and diced

½ cup low-sodium chicken broth (page 154) or vegetable broth

Select the **Sauté** setting on the Instant pot and melt the butter. Add the leek and salt and sauté for about 4 minutes, until softened. Add the cabbage and cook, stirring, for about 2 minutes, until wilted a bit. Add the potatoes, carrots, parsnips, rutabaga, and broth and stir well.

Secure the lid and set the Pressure Release to **Sealing**. Press the **Cancel** button to reset the cooking program, then select the **Manual** setting and set the cooking time for 5 minutes at high pressure.

Perform a quick release by moving the Pressure Release to **Venting**. At this point, you can either continue with the recipe or leave the vegetables on the **Keep Warm** setting for up to 10 hours.

Open the pot and, wearing a pair of heat-resistant mitts, lift out the inner pot. Using a potato masher, roughly mash the vegetables, then stir to mix well. Taste for seasoning and add more salt if needed. Transfer to a serving bowl and serve hot.

NOTE You can leave out the cabbage or replace it with 1 bunch kale, collards, mustard greens, or other dark, leafy green. You can also vary the other vegetables as you like. For example, you can use a higher proportion of potatoes for a denser dish, or you can go with all carrots, omitting the parsnips and rutabaga, for a milder flavor.

MAPLE MASHED SWEET POTATOES

A sweet and comforting side dish, these sweet potatoes will please everyone at the table. Use a rich, dark pure maple syrup for maximum maple flavor. Serve the potatoes as a weeknight side dish, or turn them into a classic Thanksgiving sweet potato casserole (see Notes).

――――――――――

Pour the water into the Instant Pot and place a steamer basket in the pot. Add the sweet potatoes to the basket.

Secure the lid on the Instant Pot and set the Pressure Release to **Sealing**. Select the **Steam** setting and set the cooking time for 5 minutes at high pressure.

Perform a quick release by moving the Pressure Release to **Venting**.

Open the pot and add the maple syrup, butter, salt, and cinnamon. Using a potato masher, mash the sweet potatoes until evenly flavored and as smooth as you like. Serve right away.

NOTES If desired, top with ¼ cup toasted pecans and ½ teaspoon of fresh orange or lime zest.

This recipe is easily doubled. Use only 1 cup water but double the quantity for all of the other ingredients.

For a classic sweet potato casserole, double the recipe but leave the quantity of maple syrup the same (3 tablespoons). Preheat the oven to 325°F and butter a 2-quart baking dish. Transfer the mashed sweet potatoes to the prepared dish and top with a single layer of marshmallows. Bake for 25 to 30 minutes, until the marshmallows are puffed and golden brown on top.

SERVES 4

1 cup water

2 pounds sweet potatoes (about 3 medium), peeled and cut into 1-inch pieces

3 tablespoons dark maple syrup

2 tablespoons unsalted butter

½ teaspoon kosher salt

¼ teaspoon ground cinnamon

CAULIFLOWER MASHED POTATOES

SERVES 4

1 cup water

1 head cauliflower, cored and cut into florets (about 1 pound florets)

2 medium-large russet potatoes (about 1 pound total), peeled and sliced ½ inch thick

2 tablespoons unsalted butter

¾ teaspoon kosher salt

¼ teaspoon freshly ground black pepper

This lighter version of mashed potatoes is a favorite of mine. It's a mix of equal parts cauliflower and russet potatoes, so you get your vegetable and starchy side dishes all in one. It's fast enough to make on a weeknight and good enough to serve anytime.

———————————

Pour the water into the Instant Pot and place a steamer basket in the pot. Add the cauliflower to the basket, then layer the potatoes on top.

Secure the lid and set the Pressure Release to **Sealing**. Select the **Steam** setting and set the cooking time for 4 minutes at high pressure.

Perform a quick release by moving the Pressure Release to **Venting**.

Open the pot and, wearing heat-resistant mitts, carefully remove the steamer basket from the Instant Pot. Lift the inner pot out of the Instant Pot and pour out the water. Return the steamed vegetables to the inner pot.

Add the butter, salt, and pepper to the vegetables and, using a potato masher, mash the vegetables until evenly flavored and as smooth as you like, then serve.

NOTE You can dress up this easy mash any way you like. For example, for a cheesy garlic mash, stir in ½ cup grated Parmesan or Cheddar cheese and ¼ teaspoon garlic powder.

To make traditional mashed potatoes, omit the cauliflower and add an additional 1 pound russet potatoes.

INDIAN-INSPIRED OKRA AND CAULIFLOWER WITH CUCUMBER-YOGURT SAUCE

Unlike most spice blends, *panch phoron* (literally "five spices") is not ground into a powder. It's a fragrant blend of whole fenugreek, nigella, cumin, black mustard, and fennel seeds, and just a tablespoon will flavor a big pot of vegetables. Here, okra and cauliflower cook in a light, medium-spicy tomato sauce that starts with toasting *panch phoron*. Accompany the vegetables with steamed rice and top with a dollop of the yogurt sauce (aka *raita*) to bring all of the flavors together.

———————

To make the yogurt sauce, in a small bowl, stir together all of the ingredients. Set aside until serving.

Select the **Sauté** setting on the Instant Pot and heat the ghee and panch phoron. Let the spices cook for about 3 minutes, until fragrant and lightly toasted. Add the chiles, onion, and salt and sauté for about 5 minutes, until the onion has softened and is translucent. Add the tomatoes and their liquid, water, cauliflower, and okra and stir to mix well.

Secure the lid and set the Pressure Release to **Sealing**. Press the **Cancel** button to reset the cooking program, then select the **Manual** setting and set the cooking time for 2 minutes at high pressure.

Perform a quick release by moving the Pressure Release to **Venting**. Open the pot and stir the vegetables to coat them with their cooking liquid. Serve hot, with the yogurt sauce on the side.

SERVES 4 TO 6

YOGURT SAUCE

⅔ cup full-fat plain Greek yogurt

1 Persian cucumber, finely diced

3 large fresh mint leaves, chopped

3 cilantro sprigs, chopped

1 small clove garlic, pressed or grated on a Microplane or other fine-rasp grater

½ teaspoon kosher salt

2 tablespoons ghee, avocado oil, or other neutral oil with high smoke point

1 tablespoon panch phoron (see Note)

2 jalapeño chiles, seeded and diced

1 yellow onion, sliced

¼ teaspoon kosher salt

1 (14½-ounce) can diced tomatoes and their liquid

½ cup water

1 pound cauliflower florets (about 1 inch; precut or from 1 small head)

1 pound okra pods (4 inches or smaller), stems discarded and cut into ½-inch pieces

SWEET-AND-SOUR RED CABBAGE

SERVES **6**

2 tablespoons unsalted butter

1 small red cabbage (about 2 pounds), cored and chopped

1 large Granny Smith apple, peeled and diced

¾ cup low-sodium chicken broth (page 154) or vegetable broth

1 tablespoon honey

1 tablespoon cider vinegar

1 teaspoon kosher salt

Here, chopped red cabbage and diced apple are cooked in a mildly sweet-and-sour braising liquid. Serve the cabbage as a side dish alongside pork chops, pulled pork, or bratwurst.

Select the **Sauté** setting on the Instant Pot and melt the butter. Stir in the cabbage and apple, coating them with the butter. Add the broth, honey, vinegar, and salt and stir well.

Secure the lid and set the Pressure Release to **Sealing**. Press the **Cancel** button to reset the cooking program, then select the **Steam** setting and set the cooking time for 3 minutes at high pressure.

Perform a quick release by moving the Pressure Release to **Venting**. Open the pot, give the cabbage a final stir, and serve warm.

SMOKY COLLARD GREENS AND CARROTS

In this vegetarian-friendly take on a classic southern side dish, the Instant Pot renders the collard greens tender in record time and the Spanish smoked paprika stands in for the traditional smoky ham.

In a small bowl, stir together the tomato paste, broth, smoked paprika, and ¼ teaspoon salt if using broth or ½ teaspoon salt if using water.

Select the **Sauté** setting on the Instant Pot and heat the oil. Add the onion and garlic and sauté for about 5 minutes, until the onion has softened. Stir in the greens and sauté for about 1 minute, until lightly wilted, then stir in the carrots and tomato paste mixture.

Secure the lid and set the Pressure Release to **Sealing**. Press the **Cancel** button to reset the cooking program, then select the **Steam** setting and set the cooking time for 8 minutes at high pressure.

Perform a quick release by moving the Pressure Release to **Venting**. Open the pot, give everything a final stir, and serve with the hot sauce alongside.

NOTE You can use any braising greens you like in this recipe, such as kale, mustard greens, or turnip greens. Because these greens are not as tough as collards, decrease the cooking time from 8 minutes to 5 minutes.

SERVES 4

1 tablespoon tomato paste

½ cup vegetable broth or water

1 teaspoon sweet or hot smoked paprika

¼ or ½ teaspoon kosher salt

2 tablespoons olive oil

1 yellow onion, diced

3 cloves garlic, chopped

2 bunches collard greens, stemmed and chopped (about 1 pound trimmed)

4 carrots (about 8 ounces), peeled, halved lengthwise, and sliced crosswise ½ inch thick

Hot sauce (such as Tabasco, Frank's RedHot, or Crystal), for serving

SICILIAN-STYLE CHARD WITH RAISINS AND PINE NUTS

The combination of garlic, raisins, pine nuts, and red pepper flakes is what gives this vividly flavored dish its Sicilian identity. Chard is one of the quicker-cooking leafy greens, taking just 3 minutes under pressure to become meltingly soft and tender. The most time-consuming part of the recipe is rinsing, stemming, and slicing the chard (reserve the stems for another use, if you like). You can save time by using a 12- to 16-ounce bag of prewashed, chopped greens in place of the chard.

Select the **Sauté** setting on the Instant Pot and heat the oil, garlic, and red pepper flakes for about 1 minute, just until the garlic begins to bubble. Add the onion and salt and sauté for about 5 minutes, until softened. Stir in the chard and raisins, then pour in the broth.

Secure the lid and set the Pressure Release to **Sealing**. Press the **Cancel** button to reset the cooking program, then select the **Manual** setting and set the cooking time for 3 minutes at high pressure.

Perform a quick release by moving the Pressure Release to **Venting**. Open the pot and transfer the chard to a serving dish. Top with pine nuts and serve right away.

SERVES 4 TO 6

2 tablespoons olive oil

2 cloves garlic, chopped

½ teaspoon red pepper flakes

½ yellow onion, sliced thinly

¼ teaspoon kosher salt

2 bunches red chard (about 1¼ pounds total), stemmed and leaves sliced into ½-inch-wide ribbons

⅓ cup raisins

½ cup low-sodium chicken or vegetable broth

¼ cup pine nuts, toasted

KALE WITH APPLE AND ONION

SERVES 4

1 tablespoon avocado oil or other neutral oil with high smoke point

1 red onion, sliced

½ teaspoon kosher salt

¼ teaspoon freshly ground black pepper

2 bunches kale (12 to 16 ounces total), stems discarded and leaves chopped into 1-inch pieces, or 1 (10- to 16-ounce) bag washed and trimmed kale, cut into 1-inch pieces

1 Granny Smith or other tart green apple, peeled and diced

½ cup low-sodium chicken broth (page 154) or vegetable broth

Use any kind of kale (or other dark, leafy green) for this super-quick recipe. Lacinato kale, also known as dinosaur or Tuscan kale, is the easiest to wash, but I also like Red Russian kale for its beautiful color and flavor. If you are looking for even more convenience, buy a bag of washed and trimmed greens. You can also swap out the apple for a carrot or parsnip. Serve this dish in the fall alongside a pork or beef main course, such as Pork Loin with Balsamic and Caramelized Onions (page 106).

Select the **Sauté** setting on the Instant Pot and heat the oil. Add the onion, salt, and pepper and sauté for about 5 minutes, until the onion has softened. Add the kale and cook, stirring, for about 1 minute, until slightly wilted. Add the apple and broth and mix well.

Secure the lid and set the Pressure Release to **Sealing**. Press the **Cancel** button to reset the cooking program, then select the **Steam** setting and set the time to 3 minutes at high pressure.

Perform a quick release by moving the Pressure Release to **Venting**. Open the pot, give the kale a final stir, and serve hot.

ITALIAN STEWED GREEN BEANS

Unlike most contemporary recipes for green beans, which serve them tender-crisp, here the beans are simmered in a tomato sauce until they are soft and tender. Romano beans, the classic choice for this recipe, or yellow wax beans can be substituted for the green beans. This recipe is also easily doubled for a big dinner gathering.

———————————

Select the **Sauté** setting on the Instant Pot and heat the oil and garlic. When the garlic begins to bubble, add the onion, salt, and pepper and sauté for 3 minutes, until the onion has softened slightly. Stir in the Italian seasoning and sauté for 1 minute. Add the tomatoes and their liquid, crushing the tomatoes with your hands as you add them to the pot. Stir in the water and green beans.

Secure the lid and set the Pressure Release to **Sealing**. Press the **Cancel** button to reset the cooking program, then select the **Manual** setting and set the cooking time for 7 minutes at high pressure.

Perform a quick release by moving the Pressure Release to **Venting**. Open the pot and transfer the green beans and sauce to a serving dish. Sprinkle with the cheese and serve.

SERVES 4 TO 6

2 tablespoons extra-virgin olive oil

3 cloves garlic, chopped

½ medium or 1 small yellow onion, diced

½ teaspoon kosher salt

¼ teaspoon freshly ground black pepper

2 teaspoons Italian seasoning

1 (14½-ounce) can whole tomatoes and their liquid

½ cup water, vegetable broth, or low-sodium chicken broth (page 154)

1 pound green beans, trimmed and cut into 1-inch pieces

¼ cup shredded Parmesan cheese (optional)

MACARONI AND CHEESE

SERVES 8

1 pound elbow macaroni

4 cups low-sodium chicken broth (page 154) or vegetable broth

3 tablespoons unsalted butter

12 ounces shredded sharp Cheddar cheese (3 cups tightly packed)

½ cup shredded Parmesan cheese (about 2 ounces)

½ cup sour cream

1½ teaspoons prepared yellow mustard

⅛ teaspoon cayenne pepper

This is a creamy, cheesy, classic mac 'n' cheese! The macaroni cooks in vegetable or chicken broth, and there's no straining or draining required. For a change of pace, switch out the Cheddar cheese for Fontina, Gruyère, or smoked Gouda.

Combine the macaroni, broth, and butter in the Instant Pot. Secure the lid and set the Pressure Release to **Sealing**. Select the **Manual** setting and set the cooking time for 6 minutes at high pressure.

Perform a quick release by moving the Pressure Release to **Venting**. Open the pot and stir in the cheeses, sour cream, mustard, and cayenne pepper. Let sit for 5 minutes to thicken, then stir again and serve.

NOTE If you like, finish the macaroni and cheese under the broiler for a crispy topping. Transfer to a 3-quart flameproof baking dish, sprinkle evenly with 1 cup panko bread crumbs, and then broil for just a few minutes, until the bread crumbs are golden brown.

SPICY GARLIC EDAMAME

SERVES 4

1 tablespoon soy sauce

1 tablespoon honey

1 tablespoon rice vinegar

1 teaspoon sambal oelek, or ½ teaspoon red pepper flakes

1 teaspoon cornstarch or arrowroot powder

1½ cups water

1 pound frozen shelled edamame

1 tablespoon avocado oil or other neutral oil with high smoke point

1 teaspoon toasted sesame oil

2 cloves garlic, chopped

Steam a bag of frozen shelled edamame straight from the freezer, then sauté them in a spicy garlic sauce. They make a great appetizer before Plum Chili Chicken (page 65) or a satisfying snack on their own.

———————

In a small bowl, stir together the soy sauce, honey, vinegar, sambal oelek, and cornstarch until the cornstarch dissolves.

Pour the water into the Instant Pot and place a steamer basket in the pot. Add the edamame to the basket.

Secure the lid and set the Pressure Release to **Sealing**. Select the **Steam** setting and set the cooking time for 1 minute at high pressure.

Perform a quick release by moving the Pressure Release to **Venting**. Open the pot and, wearing heat-resistant mitts, remove the steamer basket full of edamame. Then lift out the inner pot and pour out the water.

Return the inner pot to the Instant Pot housing. Press the **Cancel** button to reset the cooking program, then select the **Sauté** setting and heat the avocado oil and sesame oil together. Add the garlic and sauté for about 1 minute, just until the garlic begins to take on a bit of color. Add the steamed edamame to the pot and stir to coat them with the garlic. Pour in the soy sauce mixture and sauté for about 2 minutes, until the sauce has thickened and is coating the edamame.

Pour the edamame into a bowl and serve hot.

CORNBREAD

Cornbread made in the Instant Pot comes out moist and perfectly cooked every time. The buttermilk batter here is classic, but you can use regular milk instead if you don't have buttermilk on hand. Make the bread, then cook a pot of Spicy Beef and Bean Chili (page 61) for a great meal.

SERVES 8

1½ cups cornmeal

⅔ cup all-purpose flour

2 teaspoons baking powder

1 teaspoon kosher salt

2 large eggs

¼ cup sugar

4 tablespoons unsalted butter, melted

1 cup buttermilk or whole milk

Line the base of a 7-inch round springform pan with an 8-inch round of parchment paper. Secure the collar on the springform pan, closing it onto the base so the parchment round is clamped in. Lightly grease the sides of the pan with butter or nonstick cooking spray. (If you don't have a springform pan, you can use a round cake pan instead.)

Fold a 20-inch-long sheet of aluminum foil in half lengthwise twice to create a 3-inch-wide strip. Center it underneath the pan to act as a sling for lifting the pan in and out of the Instant Pot. Pour 1½ cups water into the Instant Pot and place the trivet inside.

In a bowl, whisk together the cornmeal, flour, baking powder, and salt. In a small bowl, whisk together the eggs and sugar. Whisk in the butter, then the milk. Whisk the wet mixture into the dry mixture until a smooth batter forms, then pour the batter into the prepared pan.

Holding the ends of the foil sling, lift the springform pan and lower it into the pot. Fold over the ends of the sling so they fit inside the pot. Secure the lid and set the Pressure Release to **Sealing**. Select the **Manual** setting and set the cooking time for 35 minutes at high pressure.

Perform a quick release by moving the Pressure Release to **Venting**. Open the pot, taking care not to drip condensation from the lid onto the bread. Wearing heat-resistant mitts, grasp the ends of the sling to lift the springform pan out of the Instant Pot.

Let the bread rest in the pan for 5 minutes, then run a knife around the edge of the bread to loosen it from the pan sides. Remove the pan collar, then transfer to a cutting board. Cut into wedges and serve.

CHAPTER 7

Desserts

LEMON-HONEY POACHED PEARS WITH WHIPPED GREEK YOGURT

SERVES 4

PEARS

4 cups water

⅔ cup clover or other mild honey

1 (3-inch) cinnamon stick

1 lemon (Meyer or Eureka)

4 slightly underripe Bartlett or D'Anjou pears

TOPPING

1 cup full-fat plain Greek yogurt

2 to 3 tablespoons clover or other mild honey

Ground cinnamon, for sprinkling

NOTE For a pretty, edible garnish, add a thinly-sliced, seeded Meyer lemon to the pot along with the pears. Leave the lemon slices in with the poaching liquid while it reduces. To serve, top each pear with a few slices of lemon.

When you quarter the pears before poaching, they nestle closer together in the pot, cooking faster and requiring less liquid than whole poached pears. As a result, you'll spend a lot less time waiting for the poaching liquid to reduce to a thick, flavorful syrup. Stored in their syrup, the pears will keep for a few days in the fridge, getting sweeter the longer they soak. Serve them with the whipped yogurt topping for a festive yet simple dessert.

———————————

To make the pears, select the **Sauté** setting on the Instant Pot and add the water, honey, and cinnamon stick to the pot. Using a vegetable peeler or paring knife, coarsely remove the zest from the lemon, dropping it into the pot. Then halve the lemon and squeeze the juice into the pot.

While the liquid is coming to a simmer, peel the pears, quarter them lengthwise, and cut away the core. When the poaching liquid is simmering, add the pears. Secure the lid and set the Pressure Release to **Sealing**. Press the **Cancel** button to reset the cooking program, then select the **Steam** setting and set the cooking time for 1 minute at high pressure.

Perform a quick release by moving the Pressure Release to **Venting**. Open the pot and, using a slotted spoon, transfer the pears, lemon zest, and cinnamon stick to a bowl.

Press the **Cancel** button to reset the cooking program once again, then select the **Sauté** setting. Leave the pot uncovered and allow the liquid to reduce for the full 30 minutes of the **Sauté** program. The liquid should reduce by about half, leaving you with about 2 cups syrupy liquid. Pour the reduced liquid over the pears, then cover and refrigerate them for at least 4 hours or up to 2 days.

To make the topping, in a bowl, vigorously whisk together the yogurt and 2 tablespoons of the honey until a light whipped consistency forms. Taste and adjust the sweetness with more honey if needed. Serve the chilled pears with the whipped yogurt topping and a sprinkle of cinnamon.

CARROT CAKE WITH CREAM CHEESE FROSTING

FROSTING

4 tablespoons unsalted butter, at room temperature

4 ounces cream cheese, at room temperature

½ teaspoon vanilla extract

1½ cups confectioners' sugar

CAKE

1¼ cups all-purpose flour

½ cup firmly packed brown sugar

1 teaspoon pumpkin pie spice

¾ teaspoon baking powder

½ teaspoon baking soda

½ teaspoon kosher salt

1 large carrot (about 5 ounces), peeled and grated

3 large eggs

4 tablespoons unsalted butter, melted and cooled

The Instant Pot allows you to cook a cake with the push of a single button. How cool is that? Cooking a cake in an Instant Pot is great because the cake cooks by steam, so it always comes out moist and delicious. The rich cream cheese frosting adds a nice layer of sweetness to this subtly sweet carrot cake. You can also skip the frosting in favor of a dusting of confectioners' sugar, or you can serve the cake plain alongside a midmorning cup of coffee.

To make the frosting, in a bowl, whisk together the butter and cream cheese until light and fluffy, then whisk in the vanilla and confectioners' sugar until smooth. Cover and refrigerate until chilled.

To make the cake, line the base of a 7-inch round cake pan with a circle of parchment paper. Lightly grease the sides of the pan with nonstick cooking spray or butter.

Fold a 20-inch-long sheet of aluminum foil in half lengthwise twice to create a 3-inch-wide strip. Center it underneath the cake pan to act as a sling for lifting the pan in and out of the Instant Pot. Pour 2 cups water into the pot and place the trivet in the pot.

In a bowl, whisk together the flour, brown sugar, pumpkin pie spice, baking powder, baking soda, and salt. Add the carrot and whisk until evenly coated with the dry ingredients. Whisk in the eggs and butter just until all of the dry ingredients are fully incorporated. Spoon the batter into the prepared pan and spread it into an even layer.

Holding the ends of the foil sling, lift the cake pan and lower it into the pot. Fold over the ends of the sling so they fit inside the pot. Secure the lid and set the Pressure Release to **Sealing**. Select the **Manual** or **Cake** setting and set the cooking time for 40 minutes at high pressure.

Let the pressure release naturally for 10 minutes, then move the Pressure Release to **Venting** to release any remaining steam. Open the pot, taking care not to drip condensation from the lid onto the cake.

Wearing heat-resistant mits, grasp the ends of the foil sling and lift the cake pan out of the Instant Pot. Let the cake cool to room temperature on a cooling rack, then run a knife around the edge of the cake to loosen it from the pan sides, and invert the pan onto the rack. Lift off the pan and peel off the parchment paper. Turn the cake upright and, if you like, use a long serrated knife to trim the top of the cake so it is even.

Transfer the cake to a serving plate. Spread the frosting evenly on the top of the cake, then serve.

NOTE For a gluten-free cake, substitute Cup4Cup or another high-quality, gluten-free flour blend for the all-purpose flour. For a dairy-free cake, use coconut oil instead of butter.

CHOCOLATE CHOCOLATE CHIP CAKE

An easy, foolproof chocolate cake recipe is great to have in your repertoire. This one is made with ingredients that you're likely to have on hand. It makes a 7-inch round Bundt cake, perfect for little celebrations like a birthday dinner at home. Top with a dusting of confectioners' sugar, or serve with a scoop of ice cream and a drizzle of chocolate sauce for an extra-special dessert.

Grease a 7-inch round Bundt pan with nonstick cooking spray. Fold a 20-inch-long sheet of aluminum foil in half lengthwise twice to create a 3-inch-wide strip. Center it underneath the cake pan to act as a sling for lifting the pan in and out of the Instant Pot. Pour 2 cups water into the pot and place the trivet in the pot.

In a bowl, whisk together the flour, brown sugar, cocoa powder, baking powder, baking soda, and salt. Add the eggs, sour cream, butter, and vanilla and whisk just until all of the dry ingredients are fully incorporated. Stir in the chocolate chips. Spoon the batter into the prepared pan and spread it into an even layer.

Holding the ends of the foil sling, lift the Bundt pan and lower it into the pot. Fold over the ends of the sling so they fit inside the pot. Secure the lid and set the Pressure Release to **Sealing**. Select the **Manual** or **Cake** setting and set the cooking time for 40 minutes at high pressure.

Let the pressure release naturally for 10 minutes, then move the Pressure Release to **Venting** to release any remaining steam. Open the pot, taking care not to drip condensation from the lid onto the cake.

Wearing heat-resistant mitts, grasp the ends of the foil sling and lift the cake pan out of the Instant Pot. Let the cake cool to room temperature on a cooling rack, then invert the pan onto the rack. Lift off the pan and turn the cake upright. (You can also let the cake cool for about 15 minutes, then unmold it as directed and serve it warm.)

Transfer the cake to a serving plate. Just before serving, dust the top with confectioners' sugar.

SERVES **6 TO 8**

1 cup all-purpose flour

⅔ cup firmly packed brown sugar

⅓ cup natural cocoa powder

¾ teaspoon baking powder

½ teaspoon baking soda

½ teaspoon kosher salt

3 large eggs

⅓ cup sour cream

4 tablespoons unsalted butter, melted and cooled

1 teaspoon vanilla extract

½ cup semisweet chocolate chips

Confectioners' sugar, for dusting (optional)

NOTE For a gluten-free cake, substitute Cup4Cup or another high-quality, gluten-free flour blend for the all-purpose flour. For a dairy-free cake, use coconut oil instead of butter and omit the sour cream or substitute coconut milk or plain yogurt.

BANANA–TOASTED PECAN CAKE

SERVES 4 TO 6

½ cup pecans, chopped

1 banana, peeled

3 tablespoons unsalted butter, melted

1 large egg

½ teaspoon vanilla extract

½ cup firmly packed brown sugar

¾ cup all-purpose flour

½ teaspoon baking soda

¼ teaspoon kosher salt

¼ teaspoon ground cinnamon

FOR SERVING (OPTIONAL):

2 cups whipped cream

¼ cup store-bought caramel sauce

Steaming this cake keeps it moist and perfectly tender, and flavorful additions such as toasted pecans, vanilla, cinnamon, and brown sugar ensure it turns out extra special. Let it cool before topping with whipped cream and drizzling with caramel sauce, or enjoy it plain for breakfast, sliced into warm wedges.

In a small skillet over medium heat, toast the pecans until lightly browned and aromatic, about 4 minutes. Transfer to a plate or small bowl to cool.

Line the base of a 7 by 3-inch round cake pan with a circle of parchment paper. Lightly grease the sides of the pan with butter.

Fold a 20-inch-long sheet of aluminum foil in half lengthwise twice to create a 3-inch-wide strip. Center it underneath the cake pan to act as a sling for lifting the pan in and out of the Instant Pot. Pour 2 cups water into the pot and place the trivet in the pot.

In a bowl, combine the banana and butter and mash together with a fork, mixing well. Whisk in the egg, vanilla, and brown sugar until blended. Add the flour, baking soda, salt, and cinnamon and stir just until all of the flour is absorbed into the batter. Stir in the toasted pecans. Pour the batter into the prepared cake pan. Then, holding the ends of the foil sling, lift the cake pan and lower it into the pot. Fold over the ends of the sling so they fit inside the pot. Secure the lid and set the Pressure Release to **Sealing**. Select the **Manual** setting and set the cooking time for 30 minutes at high pressure.

Let the pressure release naturally for 10 minutes, then move the Pressure Release to **Venting** to release any remaining steam. Open the pot, taking care not to drip condensation from the lid onto the bread. Wearing heat-resistant mitts, grasp the ends of the foil sling and lift the cake pan out of the pot.

Run a knife around the edge of the cake to loosen it from the pan sides, then invert the pan onto a cooling rack. Lift off the pan, peel off the parchment, and turn the cake right side up. Serve warm or at room temperature, cut into wedges, or top the cooled cake with whipped cream and drizzle with caramel sauce.

BLUEBERRY BREAD PUDDING

2 large eggs

1¾ cups whole milk

1 teaspoon vanilla extract

⅓ cup organic cane sugar

½ teaspoon ground cinnamon, plus more for sprinkling on top

1 teaspoon finely grated lemon zest (from ½ large lemon)

4 cups cubed artisanal bread (8 ounces)

1 cup fresh or thawed frozen blueberries

This not-too-sweet dessert can also be served as a brunch dish. Use fresh blueberries when they are in season and frozen ones the rest of the year. Because the pudding is steamed, it comes out very moist, which means you don't need any sauce or glaze. My favorite bread for this recipe is Italian Pugliese. With a crumb denser and softer than that of a French baguette, it gives the pudding a nice balance of tender and chewy textures.

———————

Grease a 1½-quart soufflé dish or a 7-cup round heatproof glass container with butter.

In a bowl, whisk the eggs until no streaks of yolk remain. Whisk in the milk, vanilla, sugar, cinnamon, and lemon zest. Add half of the bread to the prepared soufflé dish and sprinkle half of the blueberries evenly over the bread. Top with the remaining bread and then the remaining blueberries. Pour the egg mixture over the bread and blueberries. Cover the dish and refrigerate for at least 30 minutes or up to overnight.

Pour 1½ cups water into the Instant Pot and place the trivet in the pot.

Remove the soufflé dish from the refrigerator and uncover it. Fold a 20-inch-long sheet of aluminum foil in half lengthwise twice to create a 3-inch-wide strip. Center it underneath the soufflé dish to act as a sling for lifting the dish in and out of the Instant Pot. Holding the ends of the foil sling, lift the dish and lower it into the pot. Fold over the ends of the sling so they fit inside the pot. Secure the lid and set the Pressure Release to **Sealing**. Select the **Steam** setting and set the cooking time for 30 minutes at high pressure.

Let the pressure release naturally for at least 10 minutes, then move the Pressure Release to **Sealing** to release any remaining steam.

Open the pot and, wearing heat-resistant mitts, grasp the ends of the foil sling and lift the dish out of the Instant Pot. Lightly sprinkle the bread pudding with cinnamon, then cut into wedges and serve warm.

MEYER LEMON RICOTTA CHEESECAKE

With an almond cookie crust and a light, lemony filling, this cheesecake is an update on an Italian classic. Serve it as is, or with a dollop of lemon curd and a dusting of confectioners' sugar for a more decadent dessert (see Variation).

————————————

Line the base of a 7 by 3-inch round springform pan with an 8-inch round of parchment paper. Secure the collar on the springform pan, closing it onto the base so the parchment round is clamped in. Lightly grease the sides of the pan with butter or nonstick cooking spray.

To make the crust, in a food processor, process the graham crackers and almonds into fine crumbs. You should have ¾ cup. Add the butter and almond extract, and, using one-second pulses, process the mixture until it resembles coarse sand.

Transfer the crumb mixture to the prepared pan and press firmly in an even layer onto the bottom and about ½ inch up the sides of the pan. Place the pan in the freezer to allow the crust to firm up a bit while you make the filling.

In the now-empty food processor, combine all of the filling ingredients and process for about 2 minutes, until the filling is well-blended and smooth, stopping to scrape down the sides of the bowl halfway through the blending if necessary.

Pour the filling into the prepared crust. Tap the pan firmly against the counter-top a few times to remove any air bubbles in the filling.

Fold a 20-inch-long sheet of aluminum foil in half lengthwise twice to create a 3-inch-wide strip. Center it underneath the pan to act as a sling for lifting the pan in and out of the Instant Pot. Pour 1½ cups water into the pot and place the trivet in the pot.

CONTINUED

CRUST

7 graham cracker sheets

¼ cup sliced almonds

2 tablespoons unsalted butter, melted

¼ teaspoon almond extract

FILLING

1 (15-ounce) container ricotta cheese

½ cup organic cane sugar

2 teaspoons all-purpose flour

3 large eggs

½ teaspoon vanilla extract

Finely grated zest of 1 Meyer lemon

¼ cup heavy cream

Holding the ends of the foil sling, lift the cake pan and lower it into the Instant Pot. Fold over the ends of the sling so they fit inside the pot. Secure the lid and set the Pressure Release to **Sealing**. Select the **Manual** setting and set the cooking time for 35 minutes at high pressure.

Let the pressure release naturally (this will take about 15 minutes). Open the pot, taking care not to drip condensation from the lid onto the cheesecake. Wearing heat-resistant mitts, grasp the ends of the foil sling, lift the springform pan out of the Instant Pot, and transfer the cheesecake to a cooling rack. Use a paper towel to dab up any moisture that may have settled on the top. The cake will be puffed up and jiggle a bit in the center when it comes out of the pot, but it will settle and set up as it cools. Let the cheesecake cool on the rack for 1 hour.

Cover and refrigerate for at least 12 hours or up to 24 hours before unmolding. To serve, unclasp the collar on the pan and lift it off, then use the parchment border to tug the cheesecake off the base of the pan onto a plate, where it can be sliced and served.

VARIATION

Just before serving, top the cheesecake with a ¼-inch-thick layer of lemon curd and dust the curd with confectioners' sugar.

NEW YORK CHEESECAKE

SERVES 8

CRUST

8 graham cracker sheets

1 tablespoon brown sugar

2 tablespoons unsalted
butter, melted

FILLING

2 (8-ounce) packages
cream cheese, at room
temperature

¼ cup heavy cream

½ cup granulated sugar

1 tablespoon
all-purpose flour

1 teaspoon vanilla extract

2 large eggs, at room
temperature

1 large egg yolk, at room
temperature

½ cup sour cream

1 tablespoon confectioners'
sugar

This is the real deal: New York–style cheesecake, complete with a tangy topping of sour cream and a sweet graham cracker crust. It cooks under pressure for just over 30 minutes in the Instant Pot, which is much faster than any oven version I've tried. For the best results, be sure to let it cool for 1 hour before placing it in the refrigerator, then let it set up and chill for at least 12 hours before serving.

Line the base of a 7-inch round springform pan with an 8-inch round of parchment paper. Secure the collar on the springform pan, closing it onto the base so the parchment round is clamped in. Lightly grease the sides of the pan with butter or nonstick cooking spray.

To make the crust, in a food processor, process the graham crackers into fine crumbs. You should have ¾ cup. Add the brown sugar and melted butter and, using one-second pulses, process the mixture until a uniform, sandy texture forms.

Transfer the crumb mixture to the prepared pan and press firmly in an even layer onto the bottom and about ½ inch up the sides of the pan. Place the pan in the freezer to allow the crust to firm up a bit while you make the filling.

To make the filling, in the now-empty food processor, combine the softened cream cheese, heavy cream, granulated sugar, flour, and vanilla. Process the mixture in about 5 one-second pulses, just until it becomes a smooth filling, stopping to scrape down the sides of the bowl if necessary.

Add the eggs and the egg yolk one at a time, processing for 2 one-second pulses after each addition. Do not overprocess the filling, or you will end up with an overly fluffy cheesecake. Using a spoon or a rubber spatula, gently stir in any remaining streaks of egg yolk. It is fine if a few streaks of egg yolk remain.

Pour the filling into the prepared crust. Tap the pan firmly against the countertop a few times to remove any air bubbles in the filling.

Fold a 20-inch-long sheet of aluminum foil in half lengthwise twice to create a 3-inch-wide strip. Center it underneath the pan to act as a sling for lifting the pan in and out of the Instant Pot. Pour 1½ cups water into the pot and place the trivet in the pot.

Holding the ends of the foil sling, lift the cake pan and lower it into the pot. Fold over the ends of the sling so they fit inside the pot. Secure the lid and set the Pressure Release to **Sealing**. Select the **Manual** setting and set the cooking time for 32 minutes at high pressure.

While the cheesecake is cooking, in a small bowl, whisk together the sour cream and confectioners' sugar.

When the timer goes off, leave the pot on its default **Keep Warm** setting for 20 minutes, letting the pressure release naturally. Open the pot, taking care not to drip condensation from the lid onto the cheesecake. Wearing heat-resistant mitts, grasp the ends of the foil sling, lift the springform pan out of the Instant Pot, and transfer the cheesecake to a cooling rack. Use a paper towel to dab up any moisture that may have settled on the top. The cake will be puffed up and jiggle a bit in the center when it comes out of the pot, but it will settle and set up as it cools.

When the cheesecake has deflated about ½ inch, spread the sour cream mixture on top in a smooth, even layer. Let the cheesecake cool on the rack for 1 hour.

Cover and refrigerate for at least 12 hours or for up to 24 hours before unmolding.

To serve, unclasp the collar on the pan and lift it off, then use the parchment border to tug the cheesecake off the base of the pan onto a plate, where it can be sliced and served.

STRAWBERRY-RHUBARB COMPOTE

MAKES ABOUT 4 CUPS

1 pound rhubarb (about 4 large stalks), trimmed and cut into 1-inch pieces

1 pound strawberries, hulled and quartered lengthwise

½ cup organic cane sugar

½ teaspoon ground cardamom

The classic pairing of strawberries and rhubarb yields a tangy, flavorful compote. This recipe uses just enough sugar to take the mouth-puckering edge off of the rhubarb, while the floral, fragrant cardamom deepens the flavor of the rhubarb. Serve the compote over yogurt or ice cream.

——————————————

Combine the rhubarb, strawberries, sugar, and cardamom in the Instant Pot and stir well, making sure to coat the rhubarb and strawberries evenly with the sugar. Let the mixture sit for 15 minutes.

After 15 minutes have passed, you will see that the strawberries and rhubarb have released moisture. This is all of the liquid you will need for the recipe. Give the mixture another good stir, then secure the lid and set the Pressure Release to **Sealing**. Select the **Steam** setting, then press the **Pressure** button to select the **Low Pressure** setting. Set the cooking time for 5 minutes.

Let the pressure release naturally. This will take about 15 minutes. Do not attempt to do a quick release, as the sugary liquid can bubble up through the Pressure Release. Open the pot and stir the compote to break up the rhubarb.

Transfer the compote to a heatproof container, where it will continue to thicken as it cools. Serve the compote warm or chilled.

NOTE To make this recipe in the DUO-80 model, double the quantities of all of the ingredients.

COCONUT CHAI RICE PUDDING

Warming spices and coconut milk combine to make this creamy, gluten- and dairy-free rice pudding taste like a mug of Indian chai. If you're a rice pudding purist, read the notes for a traditional variation.

SERVES 6

1 cup medium-grain white rice (see Note)

1½ cups water

1 (13½-ounce) can coconut milk

½ cup sugar

½ teaspoon kosher salt

½ teaspoon ground ginger

½ teaspoon ground cinnamon, plus more for sprinkling on top

¼ teaspoon ground cardamom

¼ teaspoon freshly ground black pepper

2 large eggs

Combine the rice and water in the Instant Pot. Secure the lid and set the Pressure Release to **Sealing**. Select the **Manual** setting and set the cooking time for 3 minutes at high pressure.

While the rice is cooking, combine the coconut milk, sugar, salt, ginger, cinnamon, cardamom, and pepper in a blender. Blend the mixture on low speed until well mixed, then add the eggs one at a time, blending each one for 5 seconds, just until fully incorporated. Set aside.

When the cooking program ends, let the pressure release naturally for 10 minutes, then move the Pressure Release to **Venting** to release any remaining steam.

Open the pot and use a whisk to break up the cooked rice. Whisking constantly, pour the mixture from the blender into the pot in a thin stream.

Press the **Cancel** button to reset the cooking program, then select the **Sauté** setting. Whisk the pudding for 4 minutes, just until it begins to bubble and the temperature reaches 175°F to 180°F on an instant-read thermometer. The pudding will still be quite liquidy at this point, but it will set as it cools.

Pour the pudding into a single glass or ceramic serving dish or into individual serving bowls. Cover and chill the pudding for at least 3 hours before serving. To serve, sprinkle a light dusting of cinnamon on top.

NOTE Sushi rice, Arborio rice, or any other medium-grain variety will work well in this recipe. There's no need to bother rinsing the rice, since any extra starch on the outside of the grains will help to thicken the pudding.

TRADITIONAL RICE PUDDING VARIATION

For a traditional version, omit the salt, ginger, cinnamon, cardamom, and pepper and add ½ teaspoon vanilla extract with the milk and sugar. You can also use 1¾ cups whole milk or half-and-half in place of the coconut milk and stir in ⅔ cup raisins before chilling the pudding.

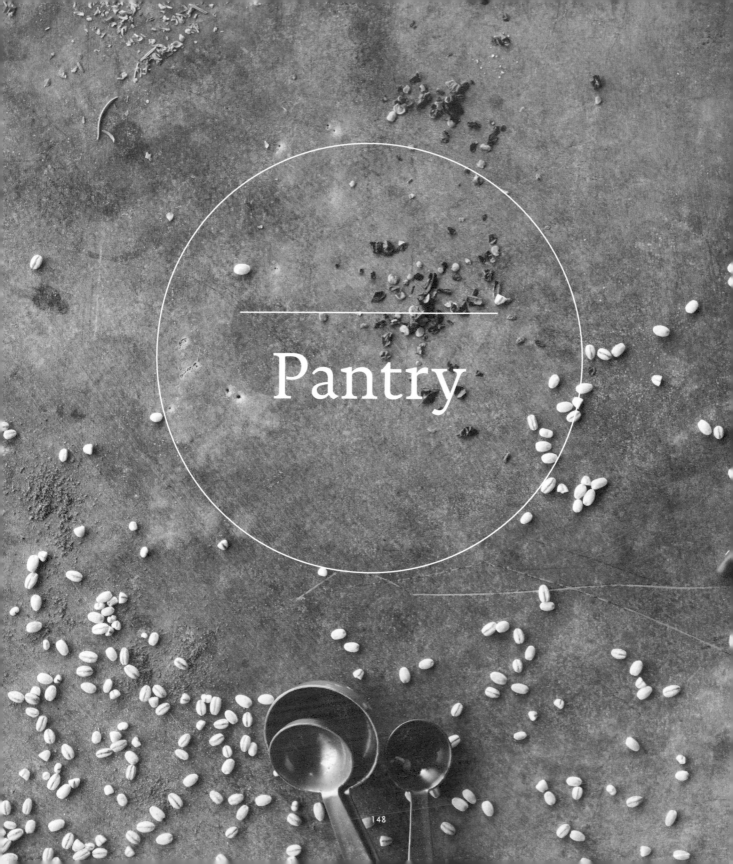

Pantry

SOFFRITTO (AKA MIREPOIX)

MAKES 4 CUPS

½ cup olive oil

3 yellow onions (about 1½ pounds total), finely chopped

8 carrots (about 1 pound total), peeled and finely chopped

6 celery stalks (about 8 ounces total), finely chopped

2 teaspoons kosher salt

———————————

Select the **Sauté** setting on the Instant Pot and stir together all of the ingredients in the pot. Cover with a tempered glass lid (or other nonlocking lid that fits) and leave to cook for 5 minutes. Uncover the pot and stir the vegetables well, then cover the pot again for another 5 minutes.

Continue to cook the mixture for the remainder of the 30-minute **Sauté** cooking program, stirring every couple of minutes. The vegetables will give up a lot of moisture as they cook.

The vegetable mixture can be used right away, stored in the refrigerator in an airtight container for up to 3 days, or frozen for future use. To freeze, let cool to room temperature, then scoop ½-cup portions onto a sheet pan or into the cups of a silicone muffin pan and slip into the freezer. When the portions have frozen solid, after about 4 hours, transfer them to ziplock plastic freezer bags and return to the freezer for up to 3 months.

NOTE If you have a food processor or a high-speed blender, it can make quick work of chopping vegetables. Be sure to process the vegetables in small portions for more uniform results.

DUXELLES

MAKES ABOUT 3 CUPS

½ cup unsalted butter

2 pounds cremini or button mushrooms, chopped

1 yellow onion, finely diced

2 teaspoons kosher salt

½ teaspoon freshly ground black pepper

———————————

Select the **Sauté** setting on the Instant Pot and melt the butter. (If the butter is cold from the fridge, slice it into 1-tablespoon pats so it will melt more quickly.) Stir in the mushrooms, onion, salt, and pepper and cook, stirring every few minutes, until the 30-minute **Sauté** cooking program is finished. The mushrooms will give up a lot of liquid in the first half of cooking, which will evaporate as they near the end of cooking. Stir more frequently as more liquid evaporates so the mushrooms cook evenly.

The duxelles can be used right away, stored in the refrigerator in an airtight container for up to 3 days, or frozen for future use. To freeze, let cool to room temperature, then scoop ¼-cup portions onto a sheet pan or into the cups of a silicone muffin pan and slip into the freezer. When the portions have frozen solid, after about 4 hours, transfer them to ziplock plastic freezer bags and return to the freezer for up to 3 months.

30-MINUTE CARAMELIZED ONIONS

MAKES 2½ CUPS

4 tablespoons unsalted butter or olive oil

2 pounds yellow onions, sliced ¼ inch thick

1 teaspoon kosher salt

Select the **Sauté** setting on the Instant Pot, adjust the heat level to **More**, and melt the butter. Add the onions and salt and stir with a wooden spoon, breaking up the onions into individual pieces and coating them evenly with the butter and salt. Cover with a tempered glass lid (or other nonlocking lid that fits) and let the onions sweat, covered, for 10 minutes.

Remove the lid from the pot. Wearing a heat-resistant mitt on your dominant hand to protect your arm from the steam, stir the onions vigorously, using the spoon to nudge any browned bits from the pot bottom. Leave the pot uncovered and set a timer for 4 minutes.

When the 4 minutes are up, stir the onions vigorously again, making sure to nudge any browned bits from the pot bottom, then set the timer for 3 minutes.

When the 3 minutes are up, stir the onions vigorously again and then continue to stir them at 2-minute intervals until the 30-minute **Sauté** cooking program is finished.

When the cooking program finishes, wearing the heat-resistant mitts, immediately lift the inner pot out of the Instant Pot. The onions can be used right away, stored in the refrigerator in an airtight container for up to 4 days, or frozen for future use. To freeze, let cool to room temperature, then scoop ½-cup portions into the cups of a silicone muffin pan and slip into the freezer. When the portions have frozen solid, after about 4 hours, pop them out of the muffin pan, put in ziplock freezer bags, and return to the freezer for up to 3 months.

NOTE The salt is important in this recipe, so don't leave it out! It helps the onions give up their liquid so they caramelize and cook down properly.

INDIAN SIMMER SAUCE

MAKES ABOUT 6 CUPS

2 tablespoons avocado oil or other neutral oil with high smoke point

3 large yellow onions, finely diced

2 cloves garlic, chopped

1-inch knob fresh ginger, peeled and grated

1 teaspoon kosher salt

4 teaspoons ground coriander

1 tablespoon ground cumin

½ teaspoon cayenne pepper

½ teaspoon ground turmeric

1 tablespoon sweet paprika

1 tablespoon garam masala

1 (28-ounce) can whole tomatoes and their liquid

1 cup water

Select the **Sauté** setting in the Instant Pot and heat the oil. Add the onions, garlic, ginger, and salt and sauté until the onions have softened, given up their liquid, and are just beginning to stick to the pot, about 15 minutes.

Stir in the coriander, cumin, cayenne, turmeric, paprika, and garam masala and sauté for 1 more minute. Add the tomatoes and their liquid, crushing the tomatoes with your hands as you add them to the pot. Stir in the water.

Secure the lid and set the Pressure Release to **Sealing**. Press the **Cancel** button to reset the cooking program, then select the **Manual** setting for 15 minutes at high pressure.

Let the pressure release naturally. This will take about 25 minutes. Open the pot and, using heat-resistant mitts, remove the inner pot from the Instant Pot and let the sauce cool.

The sauce can be used right away or transferred to an airtight container and refrigerated for up to 3 days. To freeze the sauce, transfer in 2-cup portions to quart-size ziplock plastic freezer bags and freeze for up to 3 months.

NOTE This recipe makes enough for three batches of Chana Masala (page 39). You can also use it to simmer on-the-bone chicken or lamb shanks. I have added ½ teaspoon cayenne pepper, which makes a medium-spicy sauce. Adjust the amount to suit your palate. Freeze the sauce in 2-cup portions for a quick and easy weeknight meal.

QUICK MAYONNAISE

MAKES ABOUT 1¼ CUPS

1 large egg

2 teaspoons fresh lemon juice

1 teaspoon Dijon mustard

¼ teaspoon fine sea salt

⅛ teaspoon organic cane sugar

1 cup grapeseed oil or other light neutral oil

To make the mayonnaise, use an immersion blender and a widemouthed pint canning jar, the container that came with your immersion blender, or a vessel of similar size and shape. Combine all of the ingredients in the jar in the order listed, then slowly lower the blender head all of the way into the jar. Using half-second pulses, blend the mixture until an emulsified mayonnaise forms, slowly bringing the blender head back up through the ingredients as you go. By the time you get to the top, you will have a fully blended jar of mayonnaise. Cover and refrigerate until serving. It will keep for up to 1 week.

NOTE Exercise caution and common sense when using raw eggs. No part of the outside of the eggshell must come in contact with the yolk or white, so crack each egg into a small bowl and check for shell bits before adding it to the recipe. If you will be serving homemade mayonnaise to the very young, to elderly people, or to anyone with a weakened immune system, consider using pasteurized eggs, which have been processed to eliminate any threat of harmful bacteria.

MARINARA SAUCE

MAKES ABOUT 3½ CUPS

¼ cup olive oil

3 cloves garlic, chopped

1 (28-ounce) can whole San Marzano tomatoes and their liquid

2 teaspoons Italian seasoning

1½ teaspoons kosher salt

½ teaspoon red pepper flakes (optional)

Select the **Sauté** setting on the Instant Pot and heat the oil and garlic for about 3 minutes, until the garlic turns a light blond but is not browned. Add the tomatoes and their liquid, crushing the tomatoes with your hands as you add them to the pot. Stir in the Italian seasoning, salt, and red pepper flakes, then let the sauce cook for 10 more minutes, stirring occasionally.

NOTE To make this a one-pot pasta meal, add 1 pound short pasta (such as penne, farfalle, or rotini) and 3½ cups water to the sauce and stir well. Secure the lid and set the Pressure Release to Sealing. Press the **Cancel** button to reset the cooking program, then select the Manual setting and set the cooking time for 5 minutes at high pressure. Let the pressure release naturally for 5 minutes, then move the Pressure Release to **Venting** to release any remaining steam. Open the pot and give the pasta and sauce a good stir. Serve sprinkled with Parmesan.

CHICKEN BROTH

MAKES ABOUT 8 CUPS

1 teaspoon avocado oil or other
neutral oil with high smoke point

2 to 2½ pounds bony chicken parts (such as
drumsticks, wings, or necks and backs)

2 large carrots, halved lengthwise,
then cut crosswise into 3-inch lengths

3 celery stalks, cut into 3-inch lengths

3 cloves garlic

1 yellow onion, cut into wedges

1 teaspoon salt

½ teaspoon black peppercorns

1 bay leaf

8 cups water

Select the **Sauté** setting on the Instant Pot and heat the oil. Using tongs, place the chicken pieces in the pot in a single layer and sear, flipping once, for 5 minutes on each side, until browned. Don't worry if some of the skin sticks to the pot.

Add the carrots, celery, garlic, onion, salt, peppercorns, and bay leaf to the pot, then pour in the water, going slowly to prevent splashing. Make sure the pot is no more than two-thirds full.

Secure the lid and set the Pressure Release to **Sealing**. Press the **Cancel** button to reset the cooking program, then select the **Soup/Broth** setting and set the cooking time for 60 minutes at high pressure.

Let the pressure release naturally for at least 20 minutes, then move the Pressure Release to

Venting to release any remaining steam. At this point, you can leave the pot on its **Keep Warm** setting for up to 10 hours.

Place a wire-mesh strainer over a large bowl or pitcher. Wearing heat-resistant mitts, lift the inner pot out of the Instant Pot and strain the broth into the container. Discard the vegetables. If you have used meatier chicken parts such as drumsticks, you can pick the meat off of the bones, discard the bones, and save the meat for another use. If you have used only bony parts, discard the chicken along with the vegetables.

Pour the broth into a fat separator to remove the fat, or chill the broth in the refrigerator until the fat solidifies on top, then scoop off the fat from the surface with a large spoon.

The broth can be used right away, stored in an airtight container in the refrigerator for up to 5 days, or frozen for future use. To freeze, pour the broth into the cups of silicone muffin pans or into mini loaf pans and slip into the freezer. When the portions have frozen solid, after about 4 hours, pop them out of the pans, transfer to ziplock plastic freezer bags, and return to the freezer for up to 6 months.

NOTE For an Asian-style broth, leave out the carrots, celery, garlic, and onion, and add ginger and shallots (dried shiitake mushrooms are good too).

For a warming Vietnamese-style broth suitable as a base for pho, include a whole star anise pod and a cinnamon stick.

Cool the broth quickly by using an ice bath: Pop out a tray's worth of ice cubes into a large, stainless-steel bowl, add cold water, and then rest a smaller bowl with the hot broth inside the large bowl. Don't try this method with glass bowls, as the shock may cause them to crack or shatter.

BEEF BONE BROTH

2 pounds beef soup bones
(such as knucklebones), shank, or oxtails

2 large carrots, halved lengthwise,
then cut crosswise into 3-inch lengths

3 celery stalks, cut into 3-inch lengths

1 large yellow onion, cut into wedges

1 teaspoon kosher salt

½ teaspoon black peppercorns

1 bay leaf

8 cups water

Combine the bones, carrots, celery, onion, salt, peppercorns, and bay leaf in the Instant Pot. Pour in the water, making sure the pot is no more than two-thirds full.

Secure the lid and set the Pressure Release to **Sealing**. Select the **Soup/Broth** setting and set the cooking time for 120 minutes at high pressure.

Let the pressure release naturally. This will take about 45 minutes. At this point, you can leave the pot on its **Keep Warm** setting for up to 10 hours.

Place a wire-mesh strainer over a large bowl or pitcher. Wearing heat-resistant mitts, lift the inner pot out of the Instant Pot and strain the soup into the container. Discard the bones and vegetables. You can pick the meat off of the bones if you like, but it will have given up most of its flavor to the broth.

Pour the broth into a fat separator to remove the fat, or chill the broth in the refrigerator until the fat solidifies on top, then scoop off the fat from the surface with a large spoon.

The broth can be used right away, stored in an airtight container in the refrigerator for up to 5 days, or frozen for future use. To freeze, pour the broth into the cups of silicone muffin pans or into mini loaf pans and slip into the freezer. When the portions have frozen solid, after about 4 hours, pop them out of the pans, transfer to ziplock plastic freezer bags, and return the broth to the freezer for up to 6 months.

NOTES For deeper flavor and color, roast the bones before you make the broth. Spread them on a sheet pan and roast in a 400°F oven for 45 minutes.

I find the best broth comes from oxtails, but they are expensive and it can be a wasteful way to use them unless you harvest the meat from the bones. I pick off the meat after cooking, then add it to Beef Shank and Barley Soup (page 59) or Minestrone (page 54).

PLAIN YOGURT

MAKES 4 CUPS

1 cup water

4 cups whole milk

2 tablespoons plain yogurt with live active cultures, or 1 (5 gram) envelope freeze-dried yogurt starter

---

First, sterilize the milk: Pour water into the Instant Pot and place the trivet inside. Place a 7-cup round heatproof glass container on the trivet. Pour the milk into the container. Secure the lid and set the Pressure Release to **Sealing**. Select the **Steam** setting and set the cooking time for 1 minute at high pressure.

Let the pressure release naturally. This will take about 10 minutes. Open the pot and press the **Cancel** button to turn off the Instant Pot.

Let the milk cool to 115°F. A probe thermometer with a remote display is ideal for this step because you can leave the thermometer in the milk and set it to go off when the milk has cooled. Alternatively, you can test the milk periodically with an instant-read thermometer. If you don't have a thermometer, let the milk cool until it is lukewarm to the touch. Add a yogurt starter to the cooled milk and whisk gently until it is fully incorporated.

Secure the lid on the pot and set the Pressure Release to **Sealing** or to **Venting** (either is fine), then select the **Yogurt** setting. The yogurt will begin to set up and thicken after about 3 hours, but it will have a very mild flavor at this point.

For a moderately tart yogurt, let it culture for the full 8 hours of the default **Yogurt** program. If you like your yogurt tart or very tart, you can adjust the program time to 10 or 12 hours, respectively.

Open the pot and remove the yogurt container. Cover and refrigerate for at least 6 hours before serving. It will keep for up to 2 weeks.

GREEK YOGURT VARIATION

To make Greek yogurt. Place a 4-cup or larger fine-mesh strainer over a bowl. Line the strainer with a paper towel, cheesecloth, or a tea towel. Pour the yogurt into the lined strainer, transfer the bowl to the refrigerator, and allow the yogurt to drain to your desired thickness. This will take from 2 hours for a lightly drained yogurt to overnight for a very thick, spreadable consistency.

APPLESAUCE

MAKES ABOUT 6 CUPS

½ cup water

4 pounds apples (about 8), peeled and sliced into wedges

⅓ cup raisins

½ teaspoon ground cinnamon

Combine all of the ingredients in the Instant Pot. Secure the lid and set the Pressure Release to **Sealing**. Select the **Steam** setting and set the cooking time for 3 minutes at high pressure.

Let the pressure release naturally. This will take about 20 minutes. Open the pot and, using heat-resistant mitts, remove the inner pot from the Instant Pot.

For chunky applesauce, use a potato masher to break up the apples. For a smooth puree, use an immersion blender to blend until smooth. Use right away or let cool, transfer to an airtight container, and refrigerate for up to 1 week.

NOTES Applesauce freezes well, so you don't have to worry about using up the whole batch at once. Freeze 2-cup portions in quart-size ziplock plastic freezer bags for up to 6 months. The bags stack nice and flat and take up hardly any space in the freezer.

If you like, omit the raisins and add a handful of chopped dried apples instead. The dried fruit absorbs the extra water needed for pressure cooking in the Instant Pot, so you don't end up with a watery applesauce.

Pot-in-Pot Cooking

To make Dijon Chicken and Wild Rice Pilaf (see page 68) or other similar pot-in-pot dishes, you will need a steam rack that measures approximately 6 inches wide and 2¾ inches tall. It will allow you to cook one food in the inner pot and another in a separate bowl, dish, or pan that rests on the steam rack above the other food. My steam rack has three legs and is made of sturdy, stainless-steel wire.

To cook rice with the pot-in-pot method, I use a Vollrath-brand 1½-quart stainless-steel bowl. It conducts heat better than thicker vessels, and its sloped sides ensure that all of the rice is submerged in liquid, which means the rice always cooks evenly, even if you are cooking as little as ½ cup. It's a great hack for cooking small amounts of rice or other grains in the Instant Pot.

Cooking Charts

These time charts* provide general guidelines. Most times are expressed as a range because natural ingredients can vary in cooking time depending on whether they are frozen, chilled, or room temperature, how large or small the pieces are, and other factors. When in doubt, start with the suggested time at the lower end of the range, test for doneness, and then cook your food for a few more minutes if needed. A hot pot of food takes much less time to come to pressure, so you will not be adding too much extra time to the overall recipe time.

Meat and Poultry

Pressure Release refers to whether you should let the pressure release naturally (at least 10 minutes or more for a very full pot of food), or perform a quick release when the cooking program has ended. Use an instant-read thermometer to take the internal temperature of meat after it is finished cooking, especially poultry. Insert the thermometer into the thickest part without touching bone. Beef, lamb, and pork should reach at least 145°F and poultry should reach at least 165°F. Refer to page 83 for tips on how to cook frozen meat.

Meat	Cooking Time (in minutes)	Pressure Release
Beef, stew meat	25–30	natural
Beef, meatball	15–20	natural
Beef, pot roast, steak, rump, round, chuck, blade, or brisket, large	35–40	natural
Beef, pot roast, rump, round, chuck, or brisket, small chunks	25–30	natural
Beef, pot roast, rump, round, chuck, or brisket, whole, up to 4 pounds	50–55	natural
Beef, short ribs	30–35	natural
Beef, shanks (crosscut)	30–35	natural
Beef, oxtail	50–55	natural
Ham slice	9–12	quick
Lamb, stew meat	20–25	natural
Pork, loin roast	45–50	natural
Pork, butt roast	45–50	natural
Pork, ribs	20–25	natural

Poultry	Cooking Time (in minutes)	Pressure Release
Chicken, breasts, with bones	10–15	quick
Chicken, breasts, boneless, skinless	8	quick
Chicken, drumsticks, legs, or thighs, with bones	15	quick
Chicken, thighs, boneless	10	quick
Chicken, whole	20–25	quick
Chicken, whole, cut up with bones	10–15	quick
Turkey, breast, boneless	15–20	quick
Turkey, breast, whole, with bones	25–30	quick
Turkey, drumsticks (leg)	15–20	quick

Vegetables

For the best results, perform a quick release for all vegetables.

Vegetable	Fresh, Cooking Time (in minutes)	Frozen, Cooking Time (in minutes)
Artichokes, whole, trimmed without leaves	9–11	11–13
Artichokes, hearts	4–5	5–6
Asparagus, whole or cut	1–2	2–3
Beets, small, whole	11–13	13–15
Beets, large, whole	20–25	25–30
Broccoli, florets	2–3	3–4
Broccoli, stalks	3–4	4–5
Brussels sprouts, whole	3–4	4–5
Cabbage, red, purple, or green, shredded	2–3	3–4
Cabbage, red, purple or green, wedges	3–4	4–5
Carrots, sliced or shredded	1–2	2–3
Carrots, whole or chunks	2–3	3–4
Cauliflower florets	2–3	3–4
Celery, chunks	2–3	3–4
Corn, kernels	1–2	2–3
Corn, on the cob	3–4	4–5
Eggplant, slices or chunks	2–3	3–4
Endives, whole	1–2	2–3
Escarole, chopped	1–2	2–3
Green beans, whole	3–5	5–7
Greens (beet greens, collards, kale, spinach, Swiss chard, turnip greens), chopped	3–6	4–7
Leeks, chopped	2–4	3–5
Mixed vegetables, chopped (frozen blend)	2–3	3–4
Okra, sliced	2–3	3–4
Onions, sliced	2–3	3–4

Vegetable	Fresh, Cooking Time (in minutes)	Frozen, Cooking Time (in minutes)
Parsnips, sliced	1–2	2–3
Parsnips, chunks	2–4	4–6
Peas, sugar snap or snow, whole	1–2	2–3
Peas, green (English), shelled	1–2	2–3
Potatoes, in cubes	3–5	7–9
Potatoes, whole, baby	10–12	12–14
Potatoes, whole, large	12–15	15–19
Pumpkin, small slices or chunks	4–5	6–7
Pumpkin, large slices or chunks	8–10	10–14
Rutabagas, slices	3–5	4–6
Rutabagas, chunks	4–6	6–8
Spinach	1–2	3–4
Squash, acorn, slices or chunks	6 – 7	8 – 9
Squash, butternut, slices or chunks	8–10	10–12
Sweet potatoes, cubed	3–5	5–7
Sweet potatoes, whole, small	10–12	12–14
Sweet potatoes, whole, large	12–15	15–19
Sweet peppers, slices or chunks	1–3	2–4
Tomatoes, quartered	2–3	4–5
Tomatoes, whole	3–5	5–7
Turnips, chunks	2–4	4–6
Yams, cubed	3 – 5	5–7
Yams, whole, small	10–12	12–14
Yams, whole, large	12–15	15–19
Zucchini, slices or chunks	2–3	3–4

Lentils

I've found that the best way to cook lentils that keep their shape when cooked is with the pot-in-pot method (see Beluga Lentil Salad with Italian Vinaigrette, page 37) on the **Manual** setting. Black and Puy lentils keep their shape better than other varieties. If you don't mind mushy lentils (fine for soup, Indian-inspired dishes, and the like), go ahead and cook them on the **Bean/Chili** setting as you would unsoaked dried beans.

Lentils	Soaked, Cooking Time (in minutes)	Unsoaked, Cooking Time (in minutes)
Beluga (black)	n/a	15–20
Green	n/a	15–20
Puy (French)	n/a	15–20
Red (split)	n/a	15–18
Small brown (Spanish)	n/a	15–20
Yellow (split)	n/a	15–18

Beans

The cooking time for dried beans can vary widely depending on how long the beans have been stored. For the least split-open beans, soak them in water for 10 to 12 hours, using 8 cups water for each pound of beans (about 2¼ cups), then cook them on the **Bean/Chili** setting in their soaking water or in 6 cups fresh water. I like to season the soaking water with a teaspoon or two of salt, which flavors the beans through and through.

Beans	Soaked, Cooking Time (in minutes)	Unsoaked, Cooking Time (in minutes)
Black	10–15	20–25
Black-eyed pea	10–15	20–25
Cannellini	20–25	35–40
Chickpea (garbanzo)	20–25	35–40
Corona, giant lima, gigantes	20–25	25–30
Flageolet	10–15	20–25
Great northern	20–25	25–30
Kidney	20–25	25–30
Lima	10–15	20–25
Navy	20–25	25–30
Pinquito	10–15	20–25
Pinto	20–25	25–30
Red	10–15	20–25

Rice and Other Grains

Let the pressure release naturally for at least 10 minutes for all types of rice and for other grains. For porridges (oatmeal, congee, and the like), let the pressure release completely before opening the pot. Fill the pot no more than half full when cooking rice or other grains to prevent excessive foaming and/or bubbling and blocking of the mechanisms in the lid. For quantities of 1½ cups or more, cook grains directly in the pot. For smaller amounts, use the pot-in-pot (PIP) method (see page 157). Use less water for a firmer texture, and more for slightly softer grains (see the ranges in the chart below).

Rice and Other Grains	Water Quantity (Rice/Grain:Water Ratio)	Cooking Time (in minutes)
Barley, pearl	1:1½–2	25–30
Barley, pot	1:3–4	25–30
Congee, thick	1:4–5	15–20
Congee, thin	1:6–7	15–20
Couscous (not quick-cooking)	1:2	5–8
Millet	1:1⅔	10–12
Oats, quick cooking	1:1⅔	6
Oats, steel–cut	1:3	10–12
Polenta, coarse	1:4	10–15
Polenta, quick cooking	1:4	5–8
Porridge, thin	1:6–7	15–20
Quinoa	1:1–1¼	8
Rice, basmati	1: 1–1¼	4–8
Rice, brown	1: 1–1¼	20–25
Rice, jasmine	1: 1–1¼	4–10
Rice, white	1: 1–1½	8
Rice, wild	1:1⅓–1½	25–30
Whole-grain wheat berries, spelt, farro, or kamut	1:1½–2	25–30

Time charts adapted from information provided by Instant Pot.

Acknowledgments

The Essential Instant Pot Cookbook would not have been possible without the encouragement, support, and advice of my colleagues, friends, and family.

To my agent, Alison Fargis, and the rest of the team at Stonesong, thank you for making it possible for me to reach this major career milestone. And many thanks to fellow food writer Erin Gleeson for introducing me to Alison and giving your helpful advice.

To the team at Ten Speed Press, thanks for making this cookbook come to life: project editor Kim Laidlaw for walking me through every step of the process, executive editor Lisa Westmoreland for bringing me into the fold at Ten Speed, copy editor Sharon Silva for her expert editing, production associate Heather Porter, and art director Kara Plikaitis, photographer Colin Price, and food stylists Kim Kissling and Jeffrey Larsen for making my recipes look so beautiful.

To Anna Di Meglio and the rest of the team at Instant Pot, thank you for your help throughout the project and for providing me and Ten Speed Press with a DUO60 Plus to feature in the pages of this book (and to use for testing recipes).

To everybody on my Instant Pot Recipes Facebook page, thank you for your readership and your input on what you wanted to see in an Instant Pot cookbook. This book is for all of you, and I sincerely hope you enjoy it!

To the South Bay Salon, thank you for your endless support, encouragement, and friendship. Special thanks to Michelle Tam and Danielle Tsi for introducing me to the wonders of the Instant Pot, to Emma Christensen and Cheryl Sternman Rule for their sage advice, and to Sheri Codiana for her recipe testing and organizational skills.

To my girlfriends Lizzie Paulsen and Nancy Tariga, thank you for testing so many recipes and giving your feedback.

To my mom, Cindy Harris, thank you for the many hours of washing dishes, folding laundry, and otherwise making it possible for me to keep so many balls in the air at once, and to my father, Larry Harris, for delivering lots of leftovers to my brother and his wife. To my brother, Dave, thank you for always encouraging me in everything I do.

Last but not least, thanks to my husband, Brendan. You're the best recipe taster I could ask for, and your belief in me is the secret ingredient that makes everything possible.

About the Author

Coco Morante is an author, recipe developer, and blogger who runs the extremely popular Instant Pot Recipes Facebook page and writes for her blog LeftySpoon. She began honing her craft in childhood as soon as she could reach the kitchen countertop, teaching herself to debone a chicken from the crosshatched illustrations in *The Fannie Farmer Cookbook.*

Having earned her Master of Music in Classical Voice from the San Francisco Conservatory of Music, Coco is a self-taught cook and classically-trained soprano. Her singing credits include a season with the San Francisco Symphony Chorus, and her recipes are featured in numerous print and online publications, including Simply Recipes, The Kitchn, and Edible Silicon Valley.

Coco writes and sings in the San Francisco Bay Area, where she lives with her husband and their beagle.

Index

Published in the United States by Ten Speed Press, an imprint of the Crown Publishing Group,
a division of Penguin Random House LLC, New York.
www.crownpublishing.com
www.tenspeed.com

Ten Speed Press and the Ten Speed Press colophon are registered trademarks of Penguin
Random House LLC.

Instant Pot® and the Instant Pot® logo are registered trademarks of Double Insight, Inc.
and are used throughout this book with permission.

Library of Congress Cataloging-in-Publication Data

Names: Morante, Coco, author.
Title: The essential Instant Pot cookbook : fresh and foolproof recipes for your
  electric pressure cooker / by Coco Morante.
Description: First edition. | California : Ten Speed Press, [2017] |
Includes bibliographical references and index.
Identifiers: LCCN 2017024761 (print) | LCCN 2017028607 (ebook) |
ISBN 9780399580895 (Ebook) | ISBN 9780399580888 (hardcover : alk. paper)
Subjects: LCSH: Pressure cooking. | LCGFT: Cookbooks.
Classification: LCC TX840.P7 (ebook) | LCC TX840.P7 M67 2017 (print) |
DDC 641.5/87—dc23
LC record available at https://lccn.loc.gov/2017024761

Hardcover ISBN: 978-0-399-58088-8
eBook ISBN: 978-0-399-58089-5

Printed in China

Design by Kara Plikaitis
Food styling by Kim Kissling and Jeffrey Larsen
Prop styling by Glenn Jenkins